Catholicism & Christianity

Catholicism & Christianity

by Jimmy Swaggart

Jimmy Swaggart Ministries
P.O. Box 2550
Baton Rouge, Louisiana 70821-2550

TABLE OF CONTENTS

INTRODUCTION

hat do we mean when we say "Christianity" and "Catholicism"? After all, do the Catholics not consider themselves Christian? Yes, they do. But Christianity and Catholicism are not one and the same.

Christianity, on the one hand, was founded not as an institution, forcing the name and teachings of Jesus Christ upon submitting subjects, but as a witness to Christ, lifting Him up before the world. Jesus said:

> *"And I, if I be lifted up from the earth, will draw all men unto me"* (John 12:32).

It was Christ, not Christianity, that had the power to change lives.

The Early Church, as revealed by the book of Acts and the Epistles, believed in and practiced the priesthood of all believers (Hebrews 7; Revelation 1:6; 5:10). All followers of Christ had access to Him by faith (Romans 5:2; Ephesians 2:18; 3:12). The church was identified not with any specific office, but rather with the assembly of believers, for Jesus said:

> *"Where two or three are gathered together in my name, there am I in the midst of them"* (Matthew 18:20).

Catholicism, on the other hand, involved two distinct changes from the beliefs and practices of the Early Church: a change of government and a change of faith.

Catholicism is basically a Roman institution. It arose from the ruins of the "Holy" Roman Empire and is, as someone expressed it, "the ghost of the Roman Empire come to life in the garb of Christianity." It brought itself to power through the glory of Rome and the name of Christ, by deception and force; and by force and bloodshed it has maintained that power.

Under Catholicism the church was understood to be no longer an assembly of "called out ones," meeting together to worship the Lord, but rather a group of persons coming under the authority of the so-called apostolic succession of bishops. The personal communion with God, and the assurance of the ever-abiding presence of Christ . . . *"Lo, I am with you alway"* (Matthew 28:20) . . . was now restricted to strict adherence to outward form and ritual.

This momentous transformation in the concept of the church involved not just a change of government, but also a change of faith. Communion with God was now possible only by communion with a bishop and the performance of certain rites. Outside of the ritual there was no salvation.

Sadly, many persons today are held captive by this religiopolitical power, which not only has been responsible for the deaths of multiplied millions of martyrs over the centuries, but is even now responsible for damning the deceived souls of multitudinous millions! In America alone there are over *50 million* Roman Catholics, and in the world, over *600 million* Roman Catholics — FOR WHOM CHRIST DIED.

God has called this Ministry to go into all the world to preach the Gospel, and certainly that commission extends not only to the darkest corners of heathen Africa, Asia, and South America, but also to the darkest corners of so-called "Christendom," whether it be the primitive backwoods south of the border or the bustling sidewalks and cultural centers of our large Northern cities. Wherever a thirsty, hungry soul is truly seeking . . . *"the way, the truth, and the life''* (John 14:6) . . . that is where . . . *''the fields . . . are white already to harvest''* (John 4:35) . . . and there we must go.

It is for this purpose that this book has been written: to expose the deception of the Roman Catholic church and to lead the searching heart to the Lord Jesus Christ.

Our hope and prayer for the readers is that the Lord will . . . *''open . . . their understanding''* (Luke 24:45).

CHAPTER ONE

CATHOLICISM AND CHRISTIANITY

 gain it is the old, old story:

> *"If the blind lead the blind, both shall fall into the ditch"* (Matthew 15:14).

I have, unfortunately, been branded anti-Catholic. I do not, however, consider this to be a valid assessment of my feelings.

I love the Catholic people with a deep and abiding love. I also feel that the ultimate test of love is to work for the eventual good (and happiness) of those we love. Unfortunately, when we truly love someone it can be necessary at times to cause *momentary* unhappiness in order to bring about long-term *good*.

This is what has happened as I *sincerely* have tried to direct my Catholic friends toward a *Bible*-based relationship with God.

To my way of thinking, the term "anti-Catholic" describes someone who does not approve of or like someone simply because he is Catholic. And I can honestly say that I have never met a Catholic I disliked. Having said that, I would like further to state this fact: I do *not* feel that pointing out errors in basic doctrine — caustic as it may seem at the moment — is anti-Catholic.

I agreed as a young man to accept the God-given calling of evangelist. In his epistle, the Apostle Paul told Timothy to do the work of an evangelist, and then laid down the blueprint for this job:

> *"Preach the word; be instant in season, out of season; reprove, rebuke, exhort with all long-suffering and doctrine"* (II Timothy 4:2).

Sometimes it is not *easy* to follow God's directions. It is imperative, however, for the minister (or anyone else, for that matter) who desires to walk in total obedience to God and His will. It is my God-given imperative (*and* calling) to reprove and rebuke — all the while with long-suffering and *doctrine*. Sometimes this is not well received so I am resigned to having my efforts castigated within the organized arms of the Catholic empire.

Still, as the Apostle Paul said:

> *"I was not disobedient unto the heavenly vision"* (Acts 26:19).

This question is far more than just a good-natured discussion on doctrine. For there is nothing more tragic than a false path to salvation — a shimmering mirage that lures men to their death as they die of thirst. I firmly believe that the primary doctrines of the Catholic church portray a fraudulent path to salvation, and I can think of nothing more *tragic* (however well-intentioned) than a *promise* of salvation that delivers *eternal torment* instead of *eternal life*.

I am convinced that many, many Catholics have been truly born again. Naturally, they will make heaven their eternal home, just as born-again Protestants will. But for every *one* who is saved, *scores* of others are trusting in a false sense of salvation, which will, sad to say, cause them to be eternally lost.

This is my only reason for writing on the subject. Even though I know beforehand that it will not produce any extended hands of love and appreciation from the Catholic *hierarchy* (nor from many of my Protestant brethren either, for that matter), I write because I feel led of the Lord to do so. I only hope and pray that at least one precious, seeking soul will read what will be presented and find himself directed toward the Lord Jesus Christ — the *only* source of salvation under heaven. For this I will accept gladly whatever vilification may be heaped upon me.

> *"Neither is there salvation in any other: for there is none other name under heaven given among men, whereby we must be saved"* (Acts 4:12).

THE HOLY BIBLE

Let us consider for a moment just what the Word of God — the Holy Bible — really is. The Bible is, in actuality, God speaking to reveal His inner nature and His design for creation. There is a self-revelation of God throughout nature, which is His creation.

The Bible tells us:

> *"The heavens declare the glory of God; and the firmament sheweth his handywork"* (Psalm 19:1).

> *"For the invisible things of him from the creation of the world are clearly seen, being understood by the things that are made, even his eternal power and Godhead; so that they are without excuse"* (Romans 1:20).

Further, the *conscience* of man is a moral guide, inbuilt by God, to tell us whether we are doing right or wrong.

> *"The Gentiles . . . shew the work of the law written in their hearts, their conscience also bearing witness, and their thoughts the mean while accusing or else excusing one another"* (Romans 2:14, 15).

It must, however, be expressly understood that man cannot *find* God through nature alone — even though nature *is* a divine witness — because man is blinded by sin and thus fails to read accurately the creation that continually proclaims the eternal Creator.

> *"When they knew God, they glorified him not as God, neither were thankful; but became vain in their imaginations, and their foolish heart was darkened. Professing themselves to be wise, they became fools, And changed the glory of the uncorruptible God into an image . . . . Wherefore God also gave them up . . . Who changed the truth of God into a lie, and worshipped and served the creature more than the Creator . . . . Even as they did not like to retain God in their knowledge, God gave them over to a reprobate mind"* (Romans 1:21-28).

This same sin blinds man and distorts and lacerates his conscience until it can no longer serve as an accurate barometer of the divine moral law. So for sinful man (and without a Saviour we *are* all sinners) there is the necessity for self-revelation from God (special revelation) *beyond* that of conscience and creation (general revelation). *That* revelation comes to us in the form of the Word of God.

The Word of God consists of two parts: (1) the written Word of God, which we call the Holy Bible or Scripture (II Timothy 3:16; II Peter 1:20, 21), and (2) the Word of God as manifested in Jesus Christ, who is the eternal Word incarnate (John 1:1-5).

To reconcile sinful man to Himself, God sent His only begotten Son, who is the eternal Word. He assumed human form in the person of Jesus Christ (compare Philippians 2:5-11):

"For God so loved the world, that he gave his only begotten Son, that whosoever believeth in him should not perish, but have everlasting life. For God sent not his Son into the world to condemn the world: but that the world through him might be saved" (John 3:16, 17).

He was (and is) the Word of God incarnate:

"In the beginning was the Word, and the Word was with God, and the Word was God" (John 1:1).

The *written* Word of God (the Bible) and the Word of God *incarnate* (Jesus Christ) forever are united, inseparable, and in agreement. They must stand in eternal unity and agreement or they are not of God! Of course, the written Word and the incarnate Word *are* of God, so they *do* stand in perfect agreement and unity.

It must be clearly understood that there is no Jesus other than the Jesus revealed in the Bible. If anyone states *anything* about the Lord Jesus Christ that does not agree with scriptural revelation, it is at best speculation, and at worst a blatant lie!

> *"I fear, lest by any means, as the serpent beguiled Eve through his subtilty, so your minds should be corrupted from the simplicity that is in Christ. For if he that cometh preacheth another Jesus, whom we have not preached, or if ye receive another spirit, which ye have not received, or another gospel, which ye have not accepted, ye might well bear with him"* (II Corinthians 11:3, 4).

> *"Though we, or an angel from heaven, preach any other gospel unto you than that which we have preached unto you, let him be accursed"* (Galatians 1:8).

Any source (be it the church, the pope, or a religious fanatic or cult leader) promulgating a statement or doctrine about the Lord Jesus Christ that cannot be supported by the clear and concise language of the Bible should be *dismissed* out of hand!

THE INSPIRED WORD OF GOD

Just what do we mean by the word "inspired"? In the strictest interpretation, "inspired" simply means "breathed." So, statements which we sometimes hear preachers use — such as "God-breathed" — are nothing less than literal interpretations of this word. By this we mean that God utilized certain men to put down physically the words of the Bible, but they did so under the *influence* of the Holy Spirit. God actually "breathed" on them as they wrote. They (and the work they produced) were God-*inspired*. They were moved and influenced within their own intellect to put down on paper (or papyrus or parchment, as the case may be) exactly what God wanted written.

Oddly enough, one of the most beautiful explanations of this is found in an encylical of Pope Leo XIII (A.D. 1810-1903), which states:

"God so moved the inspired writers by His super-natural operation that He incited them to write, and assisted them in their writing so that they correctly con-ceived, accurately wrote down, and truthfully expressed all that He intended and only what He intended; and only thus can God be the author of the Bible."

Does this suggest some form of *mechanical* dictation by God, where men functioned as little more than robot tape recorders? No, all human instruments of God retain their individual personality and writing ability. But these men were *overshadowed* by the Spirit of God, even to their choice of specific words. In this way their manuscripts were free of error doctrinally, historically, geograph-ically, scientifically, or whatever. This is what is meant (and correctly so) that the Holy Bible is inerrant.

> *"All scripture is given by inspiration of God, and is profitable for doctrine, for reproof, for correction, for instruction in righteousness"*
> (II Timothy 3:16).

> *"We have also a more sure word of prophecy; whereunto ye do well that ye take heed, as unto*

*a light that shineth in a dark place, until the
day dawn, and the day star arise in your hearts:
Knowing this first, that no prophecy of the scripture is of any private interpretation. For the
prophecy came not in old time by the will of
man: but holy men of God spake as they were
moved by the Holy Ghost''* (II Peter 1:19-21).

The entirety of the Bible is true, trustworthy, and
dependable — even in matters not directly related to
doctrine or salvation. (It is also interesting that the Bible,
although physically set down by *scores* of individuals of
widely varying backgrounds and experience and over a
span of millennia, has a cohesive, recognizable meter and
style that cannot be mistaken — even when read or heard
out of context.)

Oddly enough, the statements concerning inspiration
and inerrancy in the Word of God are accepted without
reservation by Catholics, Protestants, and all of
Evangelical Christianity.

It should be noted, as a qualification of the above
statement, that Evangelical Christianity is back-pedaling
in this area. Certain liberal elements are making efforts to
soften the formerly firm stand on biblical inerrancy.

It may also be noted that while *official* Roman Catholicism continues to affirm the principle of scriptural inerrancy, there is a large percentage — perhaps even a
majority — of Catholic priests (especially in these modern
times and in certain orders) who are finding their beliefs
eroded in this area.

When faith in inspiration and inerrancy are destroyed
by liberal concepts, the churches accepting these apostate
(liberal) views inevitably find themselves bereft of divine
guidance through the Holy Spirit. The result is always

coldness, indifference, and social busyness (not to mention such spiritual aberrations as liberation theology) and a marked indifference to the proclamation of God's message of salvation through the blood of Jesus Christ.

INTELLECTUALISM

Some "great, intellectual theologians" state that the Bible is not an "intellectual certainty."

I do not believe this is true.

The word "intellectual" here infers knowing of a *certainty* — as opposed to sensing, thinking, or feeling. So, while their statement may hold *technical* truth, it misses the whole point of a relationship with God.

Their statement derives from the fact (and it *is* a fact) that the Bible cannot be understood on an intellectual basis alone; there must be an underlying faith in God before His written Word becomes "quickened" (brought to life) in our heart. And this can only be brought about through the power of the Holy Spirit acting on our intellect and will.

> *"It is the spirit that quickeneth; the flesh profiteth nothing: the words that I speak unto you, they are spirit, and they are life"* (John 6:63).

> *"For the word of God is quick, and powerful, and sharper than any twoedged sword, piercing even to the dividing asunder of soul and spirit, and of the joints and marrow, and is a discerner of the thoughts and intents of the heart"* (Hebrews 4:12).

Elsewhere we read:

> *"God hath dealt to every man the measure*
> *of faith"* (Romans 12:3).

It is through this specific (albeit, small) measure of faith that man can accept the *beginnings* of believing in God, and this is what eventually burgeons into a full understanding of the person of Christ and the Word of God. Naturally this comes through faith, and it comes automatically at every person's salvation experience.

So anyone who tries strictly through intellect (undergirded often with a preconceived skepticism) to understand the Word of God on a cold, rational basis is almost surely doomed to fail. On the other hand, those persons with *true* intellect, who come armed with an underlying desire to know truth (or at least with an unbiased neutrality in their position) will almost surely find themselves coming away from their investigation as Bible believers.

AREAS OF AGREEMENT

We have already alluded to two areas of agreement between Roman Catholicism and Evangelical Christianity: (1) The Bible is truly God's Word — His written revelation to man, and (2) The Bible is inspired and inerrant.

A BASIC FLAW
IN ROMAN CATHOLIC TEACHING

The primary Roman Catholic teaching on the inspiration and inerrancy of the Bible is sound. But immediately a Roman fallacy intrudes. The church teaches (and this has been reaffirmed as recently as the Second Vatican Council) that *"there is but one revelation from God, but it has two sources*: the first is written — which is the Bible, and the second is the 'traditions' of the living church.''

Here we have an obvious (and awesome) contradiction. The Bible has been officially endorsed by the Catholic church as the inspired, infallible Word of God. But then an adulterant is allowed to intrude which is, in fact, *the basis for all Roman Catholic error*!

This is *tradition*!

The end result is that the (humanly inspired) traditions of the church not only are placed *on parity* with the genuine Word of God, but they are actually given *precedence over* it! When tradition and God's Word fail to agree, the Roman Catholic church chooses — without fail — to accept their human traditions and *reject* the true Word of God!

SOME SPECIFICS

Let us look at the doctrines of the Immaculate Conception (of Mary) and the Assumption of the Virgin Mary (into heaven).

The Immaculate Conception of Mary does *not*, despite widespread belief to the contrary, insist that Mary was *also* born of a virgin. It states that Mary was *uniquely*, in all the aeons of human history, the only person born without original sin (the legacy of sin brought to us all by Adam). The Catholic church, by declaring Mary to be born without the human inclination to sin, makes her, in effect, divine — thereby constructing a quadrinity to replace the traditional Trinity. It adheres tenaciously to this doctrine despite the irrefutable proof presented by Mary's own words:

> *"My soul doth magnify the Lord, And my spirit hath rejoiced in God my Saviour"* (Luke 1:47).

Here Mary stated her actual *need* for a Saviour, certifying herself to be human and, therefore, a sinner.

Also, there is the matter of Mary being *suddenly* taken bodily into heaven. (We say "suddenly" because no one knew about Mary's physical "translation" before it was unexpectedly announced by the Vatican in 1950.)

The Bible *does* speak of *two* human beings who *were* translated (taken up bodily), but these were Elijah and Enoch. Unfortunately, there is not a *hint* in Scripture of Mary having joined this illustrious company. Again, however, as is often the case, church officials within the Catholic faith do not let this trouble them. Once a new doctrine has been announced *ex cathedra*, it becomes "gospel truth" forever — even when the announced fact contradicts the *real* truth in the *real* Gospel.

Then, there is the sacrifice of the Mass. Again, we have here a basic Catholic doctrine, yet it is totally contrary to what is taught in the Bible.

Further, there is papal infallibility, which has no basis or hint of scriptural approval. As a matter of fact, when Cornelius, a God-fearing man, fell down at his feet, Peter (who is claimed by the Catholic hierarchy as the prototype for all popes) told him:

> *"Stand up; I myself also am a man"* (Acts 10:26).

There is no hint of papal infallibility here.

Despite the fact that none of these beliefs have any basis within Scripture, each is embraced as official doctrine of the Catholic church. And, as stated, not only are these doctrines not scriptural, but they also teach a false way to salvation:

> *"Jesus saith unto him, I am the way, the truth, and the life: no man cometh unto the Father, but by me"* (John 14:6).

*"Verily, verily, I say unto you, I am the door
of the sheep . . . . He that entereth not by the
door into the sheepfold, but climbeth up some
other way, the same is a thief and a robber . . . .
I am the door: by me if any man enter in, he shall
be saved"* (John 10:7, 1, 9).

As there is only *one way* to salvation (as delineated any
number of places in the Bible), any other system or method
will cause untold millions of people to die lost. Obviously,
church (human) tradition has taken precedence over the
Word of God within the Catholic church, with awesome
and eternal suffering the end product of adherence to such
policies.

THE APOCRYPHA

The authorized version of the Bible consists of sixty-
six books — from Genesis to Revelation. In the Catholic
Bible, however, some of these books do not appear and
other books are added. These spurious writings are considered
by the Catholic church to be the Word of God. Eleven of
these writings have been accepted by the Catholic church
as inspired by God and are included in the Roman Catholic
canon. As such, they are found within the Douay Version,
which is the accepted Catholic Bible.

We believe these books are false, and here are the
reasons why:

- As far as the Old Testament was concerned, these
  particular books were *not* included in the Hebrew
  canon of Scripture.

- None of these spurious writings (the Apocrypha)
  were ever quoted by the Lord Jesus Christ, the

Apostle Paul, or any of the other writers in the New Testament. They did frequently quote from other books included within the canon of Scripture.

- Josephus, the widely respected Hebrew historian, expressly excluded them.

- Divine inspiration is claimed by none of them.

- The books known as the Apocrypha have historical, geographical, and chronological errors.

- For the most part, they teach and uphold doctrines that are contrary to Scripture. For instance, lying is sanctioned in certain cases, magic is advocated and practiced in others.

- As literature they are considered to be myth and legend.

- Their spiritual (and even moral) content is far below the standard of either the Old Testament or the New Testament.

- In comparison to the Old Testament, the majority of these questionable books were written much later than those considered to be authoritative and inspired.

So, the Roman Catholic church has added books to the generally accepted Bible and has officially declared these books to be God-breathed and God-inspired, when obviously they are not.

THE CATHOLIC CHURCH HAS ATTEMPTED TO KEEP THE BIBLE FROM HER MEMBERS

In pre-Reformation days, attempts by bold, individual Catholics to translate and widely distribute the Bible in the common language were met with violent and harsh opposition from those in power within the Catholic church. During the Protestant Reformation, reformers (who did bring the Bible to the people in the common languages of their areas) left the Roman authorities aghast and violently opposed to such efforts.

During modern times the Roman church, in a lukewarm concession to common views, has made the Bible available to its people, but has done little to encourage Bible reading or to develop real Bible knowledge among practicing Catholics — even though it professes to believe in the inspiration and inerrancy of the Word of God.

In fact, in many countries where the Catholic church holds a dominant position, reading or distributing the Bible is still discouraged. Consequently, lay Catholics — and, sorry to say, most priests — remain totally ignorant of the Word of God. They know a few isolated verses (and these, more often than not, out of context), which are chosen for distribution to the laity because they *appear* to support Catholic doctrine. Otherwise, the Bible remains an almost totally unknown book to the average Catholic.

We have received scores of letters from individual Catholics who have questioned their priest about particular passages or doctrines and have been told that they do not *need* to try to interpret the Word of God for themselves; the priest will do it for them. Consequently, they are *still* actively discouraged from reading anything in the Bible, and the reason they are discouraged is that (as previously stated) the Word of God is frequently in *direct opposition* to Catholic traditions and beliefs. If the average Catholic finds this out, it *can* be disturbing to him.

The Catholic church teaches that the layman should not read the Bible as it may disturb him, but they do not go into any depth of detail on just *what* may disturb him. The sad fact is that the average priest, who is *supposed* to interpret the Bible for his flock, knows little more about it than the layman.

To be brutally frank, I am sure there must be *some* priests *some*where who do have *some* Bible knowledge, but I have never met one personally. They are trained in Roman Catholic *tradition*, but they are not trained in the Word of God. Sadly, it would do little good if they were given Bible training, simply because *most priests are not saved*!

The average priest has never met the Lord Jesus Christ as his own personal Saviour. As a consequence, his training and orientation are intellectual rather than spiritual. So what we find, even when the priest does endeavor to share the Word with the laity, is rather a shared *ignorance* — which can be catastrophic.

Again, it is the old, old story:

> *"Can the blind lead the blind? shall they not both fall into the ditch?"* (Luke 6:39).

I believe the foregoing demonstrates why so many Catholic Charismatics deviate so far from Scripture when they receive "experiences of the Spirit" to replace the written Word. For example, Catholic Charismatics often give utterances in tongues which, in the interpretation, exhort their followers to be more faithful to *Mary*. In the written Word of God we find, however (and, here again, based on the words of our ultimate spiritual authority, Jesus Christ):

> *"When the Comforter [the Holy Spirit] is come, whom I will send unto you from the Father, even the Spirit of truth, which proceedeth from the Father, he shall testify of me"* (John 15:26).

Quite obviously, these supposed spiritual manifestations are being generated out of the mind of the speaker and not from the promptings of the Holy Spirit.

Why is this so common? Because the Catholic Charismatic rarely has any solid biblical grounding on which to judge his relationship with God. Therefore, these "experiences of the Spirit" (which are *not* the Holy Spirit) go in all directions. Every "experience of the Spirit" must be based (and judged) on the Word of God:

> *"In the law it is written, With men of other tongues and other lips will I speak unto this people . . . . How is it then, brethren? when ye come together, every one of you hath a psalm, hath a doctrine, hath a tongue, hath a revelation, hath an interpretation. Let all things be done unto edifying. If any man speak in an unknown tongue, let it be by two, or at the most by three, and that by course; and let one interpret . . . . Let the prophets speak two or three, and let the other judge . . . . The spirits of the prophets are subject to the prophets"*
> (I Corinthians 14:21-32).

THE INFALLIBLE INTERPRETER OF THE BIBLE

As practiced within Roman Catholicism, the Bible is a captive of the institutional church hierarchy. There is no room whatsoever for the marvelous operation of the Holy Spirit, who illuminates the believer and quickens the Word to him as *He* empowers that believer to discern and interpret.

Instead, we have the Catholic church which considers itself to be infallible in its interpretation of the Bible, acting as the ultimate and unquestionable authority over its *own* pronouncements. We thus have a situation where the same body who *issues* statements *certifies* them as scriptural — even when they are obviously direct *contradictions* of the Word of God! When this unusual situation is pointed out to Catholic authorities, however, they simply state that the church is infallible.

So where is the problem?

The problem obviously lies in the fact that individuals are actively discouraged from delving into God's Word themselves — and thus developing a personal relationship with Jesus Christ. Instead they are advised to leave this "potentially dangerous" or "potentially disturbing" practice to the "experts." When they do, they then are delivered a product that is certified by the same people who prepared it. Is it surprising that hundreds of millions of people are led astray?

THE CATHOLIC PEOPLE, SADLY, ARE NOT A "PEOPLE OF THE BOOK"

The Word of God has to be the foundation for all religious beliefs. If it is not, any kind of bizarre deviation can be made to appear as solid asphalt for those trying to find the road to God. Basically this is the problem within the Catholic church. It has almost totally abandoned God's Word (if it ever knew it). Church tradition has become the foundational underpinning for all Catholic tenets of belief. And where the foundation is rotten, all else is suspect.

One former Catholic priest stated, *"I do not ever recall seeing a Bible in any Catholic grade school I attended."* He went on to say that the first Bible he *ever* saw was carried by a Protestant youngster as he made his way to Sunday school. Actually the Bible (in practice if not in principle) is effectively excluded from all Catholic worship; that is, with the exception of those brief and safe passages read every Sunday as "the Gospel."

In conclusion, the foundational beliefs of the Catholic church are built not on the Word of God, but on the traditions of men. Having made a number of statements that the liberal press and the Catholic hierarchy will seize upon as anti-Catholic, rather than close this chapter with something out of my own mind, I will quote the ultimate authority on all spiritual matters, Jesus Christ:

> *"Full well ye reject the commandment of God, that ye may keep your own tradition"* (Mark 7:9).

And as the Psalmist David said:

> *"Thy word is a lamp unto my feet, and a light unto my path"* (Psalm 119:105).

CHAPTER
TWO

THE
POPE

 ## AS PETER THE FIRST POPE?

The pope of Rome stands as the nominal head of all Roman Catholic worship. He represents (according to Catholic doctrine) the central authority of Christ's church on earth and is claimed to be successor in this position to the Apostle Peter. According to Catholic tenets, Christ appointed Peter the first pope. Peter then went to Rome where he served in this capacity for some twenty-five (or more) years.

Beginning with Simon Peter, the Catholic church traces an unbroken succession right down to this day. And *upon* this claim, the entire framework of Catholicism is built. It is therefore incumbent upon anyone honestly seeking truth to *ask some questions* before blindly accepting such critically important assertions.

- Does the Holy Word of God reveal that Christ ordained one man to be above all others in His church?

- Can we find any scriptural authority for an *organization* in which one man (a pope) serves as the supreme head?

- Did early Christians recognize Peter as the pope, or leader, of the church?

THE POPE AND THE CATHOLIC CHURCH

Here is what the Catholic church says about the pope:

"The Roman pontiff, when he speaks ex cathedra — that is, when in the exercise of his office as pastor and teacher of all Christians he defines . . . a doctrine of faith or morals to be held by the whole church — is, by reason of divine assistance promised to him in blessed Peter, possessed of that infallibility . . . and consequently such definitions of the Roman pontiff are irreformable."

In other words, the Catholic church believes the pope to be *infallible* when teaching on matters of faith and morals and when speaking authoritatively (ex cathedra — from the chair of Peter) as the vicar of Christ on earth.

Any person of average intelligence who is even *superficially* conversant with the New Testament can protest that no such ordered hierarchical system is even *suggested* within Scripture. Only the loosest and most tenuous of authority structures (other than submission to Christ, the Head) can be detected within the pages of the Holy Bible. Knowledgeable Christians search in vain for any evidence of Peter's acting as an authority figure within the New Testament Church — as the *true* beginnings of Christ's church are recorded in the book of Acts.

The other apostles in no way deferred to Peter. When the apostles and elders met in Jerusalem (Acts 15:6) to debate how to heal the first major doctrinal schism within the young church, it was James, the Lord's brother, who was obviously in charge (Acts 15:13). Peter spoke during this meeting, as did others, but it was *James* who handed down the decision.

Where is Peter here demonstrating his capacity for infallible decisions and pronouncements as an example for all subsequent popes? The decision finally reached at this time came *not through* Peter, nor was this decision transmitted throughout the church *by* Peter. The *"apostles and elders, with the whole church,"* sent Paul, Barnabas, Jude, and Silas to announce the determination of this question by the council (Acts 15:22).

It is easy enough to see from this single incident that the Early Church functioned in a manner radically different from that claimed within Catholic theology.

WAS PETER EVER IN ROME?

Peter *may* have passed through or visited Rome at some time, but there is not a hint of scriptural evidence to confirm this. (Furthermore, outside of much-quoted, Catholic "traditions," neither is there any *historical* evidence of Peter's presence in Rome.)

As Paul closed out the book of Romans (his letter to the church at Rome), he mentioned *many* people. In fact, Romans 16 consists of little more than a lengthy list of those he greeted there. Now according to the papal catalog of bishops of Rome, Peter was in Rome at this time. Amazingly, however, *Paul did not send greetings to Peter!*

Since Peter was not mentioned here by Paul, it can be concluded with some certainty that he *was not there at that time*! This, of course, undermines the very *foundation* of the claimed apostolic succession of the Roman bishops. If

Peter had been in Rome as bishop (as the Roman Catholic church claims), he would have been the first one to whom Paul would have referred! It is therefore a waste of time to consider such a groundless theory. To be frank, it is unlikely that Peter ever even *saw* the city of Rome in his lifetime!

We do know a number of things about Simon Peter, however. He was one of the Twelve. He was a native fisherman of Bethsaida when the Lord called him. He was a married man (Matthew 8:14; I Corinthians 9:5). He had no headship over the entire church. He ministered *primarily* to Jews (Galatians 2:7). And it seems he was not even the head of the *Jewish* sector of the church, much less that of the Gentiles (Acts 15; II Corinthians 11:28; Galatians 2:6-21).

Peter was only one elder among many (I Peter 5). As previously mentioned, there is not the slightest indication that he ever set foot in Rome. Instead of traveling west (toward Rome), we find Peter in the east writing an epistle from Babylon (I Peter 5:13). Furthermore, we know nothing of his death — other than the prophecy given in John 21:18, 19.

Some claim that Peter's reference to Babylon in I Peter actually refers to Rome. This is a ridiculous assertion, however. The city of Babylon still existed when Peter wrote this. It was home to many Jews and was well-known as a major city on the Euphrates River. The great historian Josephus wrote of Babylon during this same period. Why then would Peter send salutations from Babylon if he was actually in Rome? This would be as irrational as a person today claiming he was in San Francisco when he was really in New York City. Sad to say, Catholic *assertions* about this do not hold water when exposed to the *facts* of the case.

DID JESUS GIVE PETER THE KEYS TO THE CHURCH, MAKING HIM THE FIRST IN A LONG SUCCESSION OF POPES, AS CLAIMED BY THE CATHOLIC CHURCH?

First, and foremost, we know that *Christ* is the head of the church (Ephesians 1:22). Peter was never the head of the church, nor is any other man — only Christ.

Second, Peter himself said that Christ was the true cornerstone (I Peter 2:4-8). He also said that Christ is . . .

> ". . . *the stone which was set at nought of you builders, which is become the head of the corner. Neither is there salvation in any other: for there is none other name under heaven given among men, whereby we must be saved*" (Acts 4:11, 12).

The church was built on Christ. He is the only true foundation and there is no *other* foundation. The Word of God says:

> "*For other foundation can no man lay than that is laid, which is Jesus Christ*" (I Corinthians 3:11).

I think it is obvious, from even cursory investigation of Scripture, that the disciples did not take our Lord's words ("*. . . upon this rock I will build my church*," Matthew 16:18) to mean that He was appointing Peter to be their pope. A short time later they asked Jesus (in Matthew 18:1) who among them would be the greatest. If Jesus had previously stated that *Peter* was to be their pope, the disciples would have automatically *assumed* that he was the greatest among them. Of course, this was *not* what Jesus was saying when He made this statement.

Furthermore, it seems obvious that the outstanding role in the Early Church was taken by Paul, not Peter. Paul wrote some one hundred chapters consisting of 2,325 verses within the New Testament. (Actually, it was Paul who defined and delivered the New Covenant.) On the other hand, Peter wrote only eight chapters, consisting of 166 verses. Thus, it seems that Paul's ministry was far more important than Peter's. The Apostle Paul stated:

> *"For I suppose I was not a whit behind the very chiefest apostles"* (II Corinthians 11:5; compare II Corinthians 12:11).

Now, if Peter had been declared the supreme pontiff, the pope, then certainly Paul would have been somewhat behind *him*. Obviously, this was *not* the case, as Paul's statement confirms.

Then, in Galatians 2:11, we read that Paul gave a rebuke to Peter: *"because he was to be blamed."*

It would certainly seem that Peter was not demonstrating infallibility in this situation, and that he was not considered by Paul to be "the infallible pope." It is for sure that today, when papal infallibility has been formalized within the Catholic structure, we find no bishops publicly rebuking the pope for his errors.

It was the Apostle Paul who was "*. . . the apostle of the Gentiles"* (Romans 11:13).

On the other hand, Peter's ministry was "*. . . unto the circumcision"* (Galatians 2:9).

This within itself is clear evidence that Peter was not the bishop of Rome (as the Catholics teach), for Rome was a Gentile city.

The Catholic church claims that Peter went to Rome *about* A.D. 41 and was martyred there *about* A.D. 66. However, as we have said, there is not a shred of evidence that Peter was ever in Rome. Certainly, he could have been, but Scripture does not even remotely hint at such.

Actually, I believe that all evidence is to the contrary. The New Testament specifically tells us that Peter visited Antioch, Samaria, Joppa, Caesarea, and other places, but absolutely no mention is ever made of his going to Rome. This would certainly be a strange omission when we realize that Rome was the capital of the empire and was considered to be the most important city in the world.

Then if we accept A.D. 66 as the date of Peter's martyrdom, this would mean that he was bishop of Rome from A.D. 41 to A.D. 66. But in *about* A.D. 44 we know Peter was attending the council in Jerusalem, and *about* A.D. 53 we know that Paul joined him in Antioch (Galatians 2:11). Then, *about* A.D. 58 (as previously mentioned) Paul wrote his letter to the Christians at Rome — and failed completely to mention Peter as among those he was saluting *in* Rome.

To put this incident in proper perspective, imagine a missionary writing to his home church and greeting *twenty-seven* of its prominent members — *while completely ignoring the pastor!*

The entire hierarchy of the Catholic church is built on the premise of Peter being the first bishop of Rome. But once we begin to *investigate* these claims, we find no evidence to *support* them. In fact, at the same time we are finding a great deal of evidence to *refute* them.

KEYS TO THE KINGDOM

"And I say also unto thee, That thou art Peter, and upon this rock I will build my church; and the gates of hell shall not prevail against it. And I will give unto thee the keys of the kingdom of heaven: and whatsoever thou shalt bind on earth shall be bound in heaven: and whatsoever

thou shalt loose on earth shall be loosed in heaven'' (Matthew 16:18, 19).

In Rome today, at the high altar in St. Peter's Basilica, hundreds of feet above the altar and carved in marble, are the words (in Latin), ''Thou art Peter, and upon this rock I will build my church.''

Did Jesus actually appoint Peter the first pope?

For hundreds of years, at the beginning of the Christian church, no one ever used these words to claim any kind of papal supremacy or infallibility. Even unto this day only Catholics do. In the original biblical text different words are used for ''Peter'' and ''rock.'' ''Peter'' is *petros*, referring to ''a pebble or small stone,'' while ''rock'' is *petra*, which designates ''a stone cliff or a huge boulder.''

In light of this, Jesus was *actually* calling Peter ''a pebble,'' and He Himself, the Lord Jesus Christ, was the indomitable ''Rock.''

''Peter,'' Jesus was saying, ''you are a pebble [with no stability], but on this *Rock* [referring to Himself] I will build My church and no force under heaven can move it.''

Peter understood this perfectly, as is demonstrated when he described the Lord Jesus as a *''rock''* while His believers are *''stones''* (I Peter 2:5-8).

The church of the Lord Jesus Christ is unquestionably built *on* that solid, massive rock, Jesus Christ.

WERE THERE POPES IN THE EARLY CHURCH?

Nowhere in the book of Acts (which is the most complete history of the Early Church) is there any suggestion of such a person or position. Only *gradually* did the concept of an *organized* church — governed, directed, and regulated by a hierarchy of pope, bishops, and priests — evolve. And even then it did so *despite* widespread opposition.

It was Cyprian of Carthage (who died *about* A.D. 258) who introduced the concepts that were to bring about revolutionary changes in worship patterns within the church.

Cyprian demanded obedience from the whole church to the bishop of Rome, who (he said) derived his authority directly from God. He made awesome claims for the episcopacy.

In the years following, this concept was gradually intruded into existing practice, and church government eventually became almost completely autocratic.

During the years A.D. 390-461, Leo I, bishop of Rome, used all his considerable powers to establish recognition for the bishop of Rome as "the *universal* bishop." It was he who first made the claim that Peter had been the first pope (some four hundred years after this *supposedly* took place).

The eastern branch of the church emphatically denied these claims. Even the Council of Chalcedon (where Leo exercised great power) refused his request to certify his claims. His assertions of papal supremacy did, however, produce a profound effect in later years.

Please note well that it was Leo I, the first bishop of Rome, who laid claim to universal authority over the church, and note also that this did not come about until some four hundred years *after* the time of the apostles in the Early Church (of which Peter was *only* one of the Twelve).

Leo's claim was enforced through the power of the Roman emperor, but even then it received only marginal acceptance within the church. Further, the doctrine of papal infallibility was not officially promulgated until 1870!

IS THE CATHOLIC CLAIM TO UNIQUE GUIDANCE BY THE HOLY SPIRIT, THROUGH THE OFFICE OF THE POPE, VALID?

The answer to this becomes obvious the moment we consider the Roman Catholic church's long history of errant and unscriptural doctrines.

If the Catholic church is uniquely protected from error by the intervention of the Holy Spirit (through the pope's office), a person can only conclude (and no irreverence is intended) that the Holy Spirit was asleep (or at least had His eyes closed) when the following occurred during the long and checkered career of the Catholic church:

- Leo I, bishop of Rome (A.D. 390-461), advocated the death penalty for heresy.

- Leo II (A.D. 682-684) pronounced one of his predecessors, Pope Honorius I (A.D. 625-640), a heretic.

- Stephen II (A.D. 752-757) encouraged the military conquest of Italy by Pepin and accepted the conquered lands as papal property.

- Sergius III (A.D. 904-911) had a mistress, and their illegitimate offspring subsequently became pope.

- John X (A.D. 914-928) had multiple mistresses and was killed in the physical act of adultery by an irate husband.

- Boniface VII (A.D. 984-985) murdered his predecessor, John XIV (A.D. 983-984).

- Boniface VIII (A.D. 1294-1303) bought his papacy.

- Benedict IX (A.D. 1032-1045) was made pope at the age of twelve. He committed public murders and robberies and was finally driven out of Rome by the populus.

- From A.D. 1045 to A.D. 1046 there were three rival popes. During the reign of Alexander III (A.D. 1159-1181) there were *four rival popes.* (Will the *real* Peter please stand up?)

- The incredibly cruel Inquisition was initiated by Pope Innocent III (A.D. 1198-1216) and was to last for some five hundred years. This was a church court whose purpose was ostensibly to root out and punish heretics. The lands and properties of condemned heretics became the property of the church. It thus served two practical purposes: dissenters who disagreed with Catholic doctrines were silenced while the pope's coffers were swelled.

The Inquisition was responsible for the torture and death of countless saints who refused to accept the practices of Rome. Any criticism of pope or bishop was immediate cause for the most gruesome of tortures and execution. It was the most effective device ever devised for stilling criticism.

Not surprisingly, it suppressed for many years the rising tide of Protestantism within the "Holy" Roman Empire. In fact, it is estimated to have been responsible for the deaths of some 900,000 confessing Christians during this period alone.

In totality, it is estimated that the Roman Catholic church murdered some *twenty million* people during the existence of the Inquisition. And a person cannot help asking the sobering question: Is this an example of the

Holy Spirit guidance that *supposedly* keeps the Roman church on its unwavering course of infallibility?

IN CONCLUSION

Traditional Roman Catholicism states that there is only one true church founded by Jesus Christ that is visible to the world. It is the temporal extension of Christ's presence on earth. It is vivified (lent life) and guided by the Holy Spirit.

It is endowed with infallibility and will last until the end of time. It cannot err in matters of faith and morals. It is superior to, and the only reliable interpreter of, the Holy Bible.

It is visible in an authoritative, hierarchical structure that includes the very vicar of Christ — the pope — on down through bishops and priests to the average layman. It is moreover a *living* organism, *"the mystical body of Christ."* Union with this organization is, in some manner, necessary for salvation.

In contrast, Evangelical Christianity sees the church primarily as the universal and invisible community of born-again Christians. The church's mission is to witness to Jesus Christ crucified and to His plan for salvation — and to foster life in the Holy Spirit through proclamation of the authoritative, written Word of God.

It sees the church in a secondary degree, with its visible congregations as a vehicle instituted by Christ to preach the Word, to celebrate the ordinances of Water Baptism and the Lord's Supper, and to gather saved Christians in fellowship for mutual edification. Its life span in sacred history is limited to that period from Pentecost to the Rapture.

It constantly renews itself by submitting to the guidelines of the inerrant Scriptures and by making itself available to the power of the Holy Spirit. No latter-day revelations are accepted if they are not in total agreement with the letter and spirit of God's written Word. It supports no intricate, external, contrived, hierarchical structure, but conforms to the pattern of the simple pastoral framework revealed within the New Testament.

It relies without reservation on God's sustaining help and claims no infallible gift in regard to interpreting the Word of God. It says the church is a saved *people* — not an organization based on the weaknesses of men.

It does not claim to save. It makes God's plan of salvation known to man at all times and in all places. It is a slave to the sovereign power of Jesus Christ, but enslaves no man's conscience. It believes all born-again people are a part of the body of Christ — His universal church.

CHAPTER
THREE

THE ROLE
OF THE PRIEST
IN THE CHURCH

 ETER, THE APOSTLES, AND PRIESTS

The Catholic church contends that the Apostle Simon Peter was the first pope and that all subsequent popes are a direct succession of this line originating with Peter. It further states that all priests are an additional apostolic succession (a direct line descending from the apostles). In other words, all Catholic priests are the successors to James, John, Andrew, Thomas, et cetera.

The Catholic church then goes on to state that priests are called Gods (spelled with a capital ''G''). The priest is a God who makes Gods.

The Catholic church teaches that if a person blindly obeys his priest, he cannot possibly sin! If what the priest commands is not correct, the responsibility is the priest's, not his. By obeying the priest, a person cannot possibly go wrong.

"God deigns to make prelates His own equals. If, then, you receive a command from one who holds the place of God, you should observe it with the same diligence as if it came from God Himself."

"Though a confessor might (by chance) make a mistake, the penitent in obeying him is secure and does not err."

A person is expected to obey blindly; that is, *without question*. He should be careful not to challenge the statements and directions of the priest lest he wander over into an area where he himself will assume responsibility for the survival of his own eternal soul.

In other words, he is taught to keep his eyes focused on one great principle: when a person obeys the priest, he is obeying God. Of course, when a person obeys God, he can do no wrong. A person should force himself, therefore, to obey his priest, despite any questions or doubts that may creep into his mind. He should suspend his *rational* judgment as he "receives by faith" whatever the priest may choose to tell him.

But what if a still, small voice speaks to his heart and asks, "But what if I am condemned to hell because of obeying my priest? To whom do I *then* turn?"

The Catholic answer? "An impossible situation. Don't even think about it."

John A. O'Brien, in his book, *The Faith of Millions*, explains that Christ is *"brought down from heaven by the priest and presented as the victim of man's sins."*

An interesting picture, to be sure: our Lord and Saviour fidgeting on His seat (at the right hand of the Father) as He awaits His next summons from some neophyte priest who will then utilize His eternal sacrifice to *exorcise* sin from some penitent.

This certainly is not the picture I have of *my* Saviour!

One Catholic stated: *"If I were to simultaneously meet a priest and an angel, I would salute the priest before saluting the angel. The priest holds the place of God."*

WE MUST SAY THIS

No priest is a successor to the apostles. The role of the priest was forever eliminated on the day that Christ was placed on the cross. *Since* then, this is an illegitimate position — *according to Scripture*! In other words, the role of priest is not recognized as such by God Almighty and has absolutely no place or position in New Testament Christianity. And the continuing condition of celibacy (as imposed by the Catholic church) has fostered untold immorality among the Catholic hierarchy.

THE SUCCESSION OF THE PRIESTHOOD
FROM THE APOSTLES

The Catholic church bases its foundational structure of pope, bishops, and priests on Matthew 16:17-19. As discussed in other chapters, Christ did not intend for Peter (or any other apostle) to be set up as the head of His church. There is only one head to Christ's church and that is Christ Himself (Ephesians 4:14-17).

In essence, Jesus said to Peter:

> *"Thou art Peter* [an inconsequential little stone], *and upon this* [eternal] *rock* [boulder] [Christ Himself] *I will build my church"* (Matthew 16:18).

Christ is the single and eternal head of His church — not Peter. Neither is the pope, the cardinal, the bishop, or priest (nor Protestant bishop or pastor, for that matter). Peter was simply one of the builders (Ephesians 2:20-22; I Peter 2:4, 5; I Peter 5:1-8).

The great promise to the church in Matthew 16:18 was given not exclusively to Peter, but to *all* believers

(Matthew 17:20; 18:18-22; Mark 9:23; 11:22-24; Luke 10:19; John 14:12; Acts 1:8). It must be remembered here that keys are a biblical symbol of *authority*. Hence, they mean *authority and power to do the works of Christ* — as are given (as stated) to *any* believer.

So, there was no inferred succession of pope, bishop, or priest in the statement made by Jesus Christ. This is a total fabrication. Of course, when a person threatens the validity of this premise, he threatens the entire Catholic hierarchy because it is based totally on this erroneous fabrication.

ARE THERE PRIESTS IN THE NEW TESTAMENT CHURCH?

There is absolutely no mention of the position of priest within the New Testament church. There *were* priests in the *Old Testament* — simply because Jesus had not as yet suffered and died for us on Calvary. The moment He did, He became our eternal High Priest, forever dissolving any need for an earthly priest to intercede with God in our place. Old Testament priests fulfilled this role when they offered sacrifices, which were then required as atonement for sin — under the rules and laws established by God for the Old Testament church. The moment Jesus offered Himself as the *ultimate* sacrifice, this *eternally* served as propitiation for man's sins — and the position of earthly priest became obsolete.

When Jesus died, He became the total fulfillment of the Law. The Apostle John expressed it so beautifully:

> *"Behold the Lamb of God, which taketh away the sin of the world"* (John 1:29).

The Apostle Paul said:

"Wherefore, holy brethren, partakers of the heavenly calling, consider the Apostle and High Priest of our profession, Christ Jesus" (Hebrews 3:1).

Paul went on to say:

"Seeing then that we have a great high priest, that is passed into the heavens, Jesus the Son of God, let us hold fast our profession. For we have not an high priest which cannot be touched with the feeling of our infirmities; but was in all points tempted like as we are, yet without sin. Let us therefore come boldly unto the throne of grace, that we may obtain mercy, and find grace to help in time of need" (Hebrews 4:14-16).

The sole purpose of the priest in the Old Testament church was to intercede for man so that he could obtain mercy and grace. As has been pointed out, this position is now occupied by Jesus Christ. Today, clothed in the grace and authority of Jesus' all-encompassing sacrifice, we (imperfect though we admittedly are) have been *justified* (through no action on *our* part) to enter *personally* into the presence of God. Where then is the need for a human priest to transmit our appeal to God?

"Wherefore he is able also to save them to the uttermost that come unto God by him, seeing he ever liveth to make intercession for them" (Hebrews 7:25).

With such an advocate, does a person feel he needs a priest to act as his agent?

> *"Now of the things which we have spoken this is*
> *the sum: We have such an high priest, who is set on*
> *the right hand of the throne of the Majesty in the*
> *heavens . . . . But now hath he obtained a more*
> *excellent ministry, by how much also he is the*
> *mediator of a better covenant, which was estab-*
> *lished upon better promises"* (Hebrews 8:1, 6).

Paul continued:

> *"But into the second* [tabernacle] *went the high*
> *priest alone once every year, not without blood,*
> *which he offered for himself, and for the errors of the*
> *people"* (Hebrews 9:7).

This was the Old Testament situation that Paul was review-
ing, where the high priest went annually before God to beg
mercy for the sins of Israel. He then stated:

> *"For Christ is not entered into the holy places*
> *made with hands* [which *were* in physical existence
> during Old Testament days], *which are the figures of*
> *the true* [which only represent the throne of God];
> *but into heaven itself, now to appear in the presence*
> *of God for us"* (Hebrews 9:24).

Does that make a person's flesh tingle? In essence, Paul
completed this thought by saying:

> *"And to Jesus the mediator of the new covenant,*
> *and to the blood of sprinkling, that speaketh better*
> *things than that of Abel"* (Hebrews 12:24).

Clearly, we are told here that the old priesthood is permanently done away with and Jesus Christ is the complete and

only Mediator between God and man. Therefore, from the moment Christ ascended the cross at Calvary, there was never again (*eternally*) the need for a priest. Today anyone who tries to intrude a priest between man and God is flying in the face of scriptural evidence.

> *"For there is one God, and one mediator between God and men, the man Christ Jesus; Who gave himself a ransom for all"* (I Timothy 2:5, 6).

There is no conceivable need for an *additional* mediator for man, and anyone intruding himself into this position is usurping authority over the awesome sacrifice of Calvary.

CAN A PRIEST FORGIVE SIN?

The following litany is the officially prescribed prayer recited by the priest when he removes sin from those requesting this service:

> *God, the Father of mercies*
> *Through the death and resurrection of His Son*
> *Has reconciled the world to Himself*
> *And sent the Holy Spirit among us*
> *For the forgiveness of sins*
> *Through the ministry of the church.*
> *May God give you pardon and peace,*
> *And I absolve you from your sins*
> *In the name of the Father, and of the Son*
> *And of the Holy Spirit.*

There are several points of interest that should be mentioned in regard to this "prayer" when we weigh the statements it contains against Scripture. To begin with, it states (in lines 5 and 6) that the Holy Spirit was sent among

us "for the forgiveness of sins." While the specific tasks
of the Holy Spirit are many and varied (for example, to
endue with power, to give revelation, to convict of sin, to
teach, *et al*), it is *not* the function of the Holy Spirit to
forgive sin. In fact, this was concisely summed up by the
Apostle Peter, when he said:

> *"Repent, and be baptized . . . in the name*
> *of Jesus Christ for the remission of sins, and*
> [then] *ye shall receive the gift of the Holy*
> *Ghost"* (Acts 2:38).

This is error *one* in the Catholic litany for forgiving
sin.

Error *two* is glaringly revealed in line 7. This says that
the Holy Spirit's (erroneous) mission to forgive sins is
accomplished *through the ministry of the church*. Now
there *is* a ministry for the church in regard to the remission
of sin, but this is, quite simply, to announce to the world
the good news that forgiveness of sin requires only one
thing, and that is acceptance of Jesus' sacrifice on Calvary.
It is *only* the blood of Jesus that washes us clean, and the
world hears about this only through the ministry of the
body of Christ. To imply (as this litany does) that forgiveness of sin requires a middleman — the approval or
assistance of any individual or organization — is little
short of outright blasphemy.

Error *three* is contained in lines 8 and 9. Here the priest
requests "pardon and peace" from God the Father, but it
is *the priest* who states ". . . and *I* absolve you from your
sins." A person cannot help wondering how God the
Father and Jesus Christ *occupy* themselves in heaven (and
no blasphemy is intended) when so much of heavenly
administration has been assumed here on earth by Catholic
priests.

One of the first things a Catholic is taught is that penance is one of the seven sacraments — "instituted by Christ" — which results in the salvation of men (or "getting to heaven" as most Catholics prefer to describe it). This doctrine states, without equivocation, that Jesus gave His apostles the authority to forgive or retain sins and that this authority since then has resided exclusively within the structure of the Catholic church.

Although official pronouncements of the Catholic church have recently (and somewhat reluctantly) conceded that an occasional person outside the church *may* be saved, one cannot escape the feeling that these statements have been delivered with a concealed wink to the faithful: "Oh, sure, someone *may* slip through the screening, but *we* know the ritual that *ensures* that you will get in: the sacraments of confession, penance, absolution, and Communion."

Priests within the Catholic church are still designated as the only bona fide bearers of this power to forgive — or not to forgive — sin. For the sinner to receive of this power, first he must confess verbally his misdeeds and the priest then imposes a "penance" (for example, the recitation of three "Hail Marys" and three "Our Fathers") and grants absolution.

To keep things moving in the confession lines, it is usually understood that the penitent will perform his penance on his own time. It is not clear whether freedom of sin comes at the moment of absolution or at the termination of the penance. Presumably, if the penance is *not* done, the absolution is canceled and the sinner is returned to his unsaved condition. It also is not clear whether there is a divine time limit on completing penance, but if a person is suffering ill health or is occupied in a dangerous job it seems to behoove the person to complete his penance as quickly as possible.

Mandatory confession of sins by a Christian to a "duly authorized priest" is so divergent from the simplicity of the New Testament that a person may be tempted to snicker at the gullibility of even the best educated of Catholics. But, as was stated by a former Catholic, a person should not laugh at a tragedy, and the loss of uncounted Catholic souls who could have been saved by Christ the Mediator *is* a tragedy of awesome proportions.

The very idea of a mortal man having the power to forgive sins is so ludicrous that even the hypocritical Pharisees of Jesus' day were scandalized when Jesus told the sick man, in Mark 2:5, that his sins were forgiven. The shocked Pharisees recoiled and exclaimed:

> *"Why doth this man thus speak blasphemies? who can forgive sins but God only?"* (Mark 2:7).

A priest is, by definition, a mediator between God and man. So, let us look further at the Roman Catholic ritual for absolving a person of sin.

Although the individual "sacraments" still consist of confession, penance, and absolution (augmented by Communion, which somehow *enhances* the forgiven state of the former sinner), there was a change in terminology connected with the most recent Vatican Councils. These are now lumped together linguistically into what is referred to as the Rite of Reconciliation.

The biblical text invoked by Rome as the written authority for the priest's presumed ability to forgive sin is this:

> *"Then said Jesus to them again, Peace be unto you: as my Father hath sent me, even so send I you. And when he had said this, he*

*breathed on them, and saith unto them, Receive ye
the Holy Ghost: Whose soever sins ye remit, they are
remitted unto them; and whose soever sins ye
retain, they are retained''* (John 20:21-23).

The Catholic church adopts this Scripture as ''proof''
that Christ gave His *apostles* power to forgive (or *not* to
forgive) sin. They then go on to state that all the powers of
the apostles have been handed down to their successors in
the church — the bishops. Priests in turn *share* in the office
of the bishop, who possesses the fullness of the priesthood. Therefore, priests have the power to forgive sins.

Actually, Rome should admit three things:

First, Jesus used the perfect tense when speaking the
words ''forgiven'' and ''retained.'' This indicates an
action that has *already been* performed. So, in more accurate translation, the account should have been rendered,
''If you forgive the sins of any, they have *already been*
forgiven, and if you retain the sins of any, they have
already been retained.''

Jesus was actually saying that sins have *already been*
forgiven in heaven, through acceptance of the proclamation of
forgiveness through the blood of Christ — or they have
already been retained, through the individual's rejection
of Jesus' sacrifice.

To be frank, millions of Christians do this every wak-
ing day as they tell those to whom they witness that their
sins are assuredly forgiven the moment they come to Jesus
Christ as Saviour. Conversely, they assure those who
reject the Saviour's atoning sacrifice that their sins are
retained (unforgiven).

Second (and this is a most important point that the
Catholic church has either missed or chosen to ignore),
this section of Scripture makes it absolutely clear that Jesus
was speaking to a group of His *disciples* (learners). It was *not* a

gathering of just the *apostles*. (In fact, John 20:24 states that not *all* the apostles *were* present.)

So we know that when Jesus delivered these words, He was speaking to a disparate group of Christians — not apostles. Of course, Rome claims that the apostles alone were the first *priests* ordained by Jesus. But here we have an unstructured group of followers to whom these words were announced. Were they not *all* given this ability (to forgive sins) if such was the authority delivered? And, if so, does this not then transmit down to *every* Christian today?

Rome cannot have it both ways. If the Roman Catholics choose to accept this as proof of the ability of humans to forgive sin (in the authority of Jesus Christ), they must also accept it in *all* Christians, not just in priests.

Now, what does the Bible say about apostles forgiving sin following this statement by our Lord? Certainly, if such authority was intended, we could expect that the book of Acts, not to mention the epistles, would address such actions as *confirmation* that this was in fact what the Lord intended; for . . .

> *". . . in the mouth of two or three witnesses every word may be established"* (Matthew 18:16).

Ah, but there is not a single instance in Scripture of an apostle forgiving sins in the manner practiced by Rome in her Rite of Reconciliation.

The Apostle Peter did *not* give absolution to Cornelius (Acts 10). The Apostle Paul did *not* give absolution to the Philippian jailer (Acts 16)! He preached salvation through the blood of Christ and opened the way for his hearers to receive *true* forgiveness. In that sense only did the apostles cause people's sins to be forgiven. This is just not the New Testament proclamation of forgiveness through repentance and faith in Jesus Christ.

Peter stated as much:

> *"To him* [Jesus Christ] *give all the prophets witness, that through his name whosoever believeth in him shall receive remission of sins"* (Acts 10:43).

Again we must state that the only mediator between God and man is *". . . the man Christ Jesus"* (I Timothy 2:5).

It should also be noted that the Early Church did not consider its presbyters (also known as bishops or overseers, which would most closely compare to pastors today) to be priests. *In fact, it was the proud boast of Christians to the pagan world that they had "neither altar nor sacrifice, and therefore no priests."* The tragic truth is that the idea of confessing sins to a priest is something of *pre-*Christian origin, having its source in idolatrous Babylonian mystery cults.

"Babel, or Babylon, was built by Nimrod . . . . It was the seat of the first great apostasy. Here the 'Babylonian cult' was invented, a system claiming to reveal the most divine secrets. Before a member could be initiated, he had to 'confess' to the priest. The priest then had him in his power. This is the secret of the powers of the priests of the Roman Catholic church today."

If a person is a Catholic and the Holy Spirit moves him to forsake the practice of confession to a priest, he should know that he will not be rejecting a Christ-ordained sacrament. He will simply be abandoning a tradition wholly manufactured by man. There is only one Person (our Heavenly Father, in the name of Jesus) to whom the Christian should confess his sins.

> *"If we confess our sins, he is faithful and just to forgive us our sins, and to cleanse us from all unrighteousness"* (I John 1:9).

Third, wrongs may be committed between two Christians, and when such is the case, James said children of God should . . .

> *"Confess your faults one to another, and pray one for another, that ye may be healed"* (James 5:16).

This, incidentally, is the *one* case where man *can* forgive sin in others. When we are the injured party, and we generously forgive the person who transgressed against us, this is forgiveness of sin (among men) of the highest order.

THE QUESTION REMAINS

So the question remains: Of all the millions of Catholics confessing their sins to priests, are their sins actually forgiven?

Of course, no human being can answer this question.

It seems foolhardy, on the surface, when we have a clear and concise system spelled out within God's Word, to follow practices that are diametrically opposed, and then hope they might work.

Quite possibly, God looks at the heart of the individual rather than at the terrible error in which he has been entrapped. *However, for every person who does somehow get through to God in the confessional, the far greater percentage receive no forgiveness.* They come out of the confessional with the same sins they carried into it.

Finally, a brief word should be said on the fact that the whole system of "drive in" absolution (delivered during a quick trip through a confessional) *can* lead to hardening of the heart against the consequences of sin. The mere fact that a clean slate and a fresh sheet can be obtained every Sunday morning (by a faceless priest behind a grill who hears and absolves the penitent of sin) can lead a person to be less than conscientious in his efforts to *avoid* sin. On the other hand, a direct confrontation with God the Father and His Son can lead him honestly to forsake future sin — and to avoid the situations that can make it more likely.

IMMORALITY IN THE PRIESTHOOD

There are two specific areas that cause tremendous difficulty in the personal lives of priests. The first is the consumption of alcoholic beverage (wine) that is required during the performance of the Mass. (This has resulted in a tragic rate of alcoholism among priests.) The second is the matter of mandatory celibacy.

Former priest Bartholomew F. Brewer tells of one of his first experiences in hearing confession. He says:

"When I slid back the door covering the opaque screen between the penitent and me, a man's voice on the other side gave the standard opening: 'Bless me, Father, it has been two weeks since my last confession. I confess to Almighty God, to the blessed Virgin Mary, to blessed Michael the Archangel, to blessed John the Baptist, to the holy Apostles Peter and Paul, to all the saints and to you, Father, that I have sinned exceedingly in word, thought, and deed, through my fault, through my fault, through my most grievous fault.' He then went on to say, 'I am a Catholic priest and here are my sins.'"

What followed was a lengthy and graphic description of one sexual affair after another. His confession was a detailed account of a *series* of seductions and conquests in rapid succession.

The Catholic church demands that the office of priest not be consistent with sexual relationships. It should be pointed out, however, that celibacy is not supported by any Scripture. It is against nature, and the Apostle Peter (who is supposedly the role model for all popes) was definitely married. Over the centuries a number of popes have been married.

The actual purpose for the imposition of celibacy on the priesthood is that Rome wishes to have total control of the labor, money, property, and actions of every Catholic priest, monk, and nun. All the arguments in the world will not dispel this one simple fact alone.

One former Catholic priest said thousands of priests and nuns would leave the Catholic church, but they have no place to go. What can the defrocked priest do? Who will care? Most of them believe that all Protestants are enemies. Most who leave the church are shunned by former friends and are treated as a disgrace by even their own families.

Bartholomew Brewer states:

"The system of celibacy is utterly mischievous and the cause of much immorality and aberrant behavior — including homosexuality."

It is certainly to be admitted that drunkenness and immorality have their place in the ministry of Protestantism as well, but I do not feel that they are even remotely as widespread as they are among the Catholic priesthood.

PRIESTS IN THE AGE OF GRACE

Is this scriptural? The term priest (*hiereus* in the Greek) is used in the New Testament in two senses: (1) it speaks of priests of the Old Testament order, and (2) it speaks of *all Christians being priests*. In no place are elders of the church or preachers of the Gospel called priests.

"Jesus Christ . . . hath made us kings and priests unto God" (Revelation 1:5, 6).

In summary:

• There was no succeeding hierarchy of popes, bishops, or priests evolving from the apostles.

• There are no priests recognized by God in the New Testament church — except as referred to in the above two cases.

• No priest can forgive sin — only God can do this. (And it should be additionally noted that Jesus Christ does not require assistance in administering forgiveness to the Christian who asks for it.)

• Celibacy, as imposed on Catholic priests, is both unscriptural and the cause of much tragic immorality.

"And he gave some, apostles; and some, prophets; and some, evangelists; and some, pastors and teachers; For the perfecting of the saints, for the work of the ministry, for the edifying of the body of Christ" (Ephesians 4:11, 12).

CHAPTER FOUR

THE MASS —
THE HOLY
EUCHARIST

 rances and I sat at a table, deep in conversation with a lovely young lady. She had a sweet spirit and the conversation flowed back and forth with obvious sincerity on both sides. She was a writer — and a devout Catholic. I think, in all honesty, that she was there to try to *convert* me to the greater truths of the Catholic faith — or at least to dig down and unearth my most basic motives.

We discussed many things, among which was the Holy Eucharist. She presented, with a hint of triumph, a Scripture:

> *"Then Jesus said unto them, Verily, verily, I say unto you, Except ye eat the flesh of the Son of man, and drink his blood, ye have no life in you. Whoso eateth my flesh, and drinketh my blood, hath eternal life; and I will raise him up at the last day"* (John 6:53, 54).

With complete confidence in her position, she looked me in the eye and stated with conviction, "But, Brother Swaggart, the Bible is emphatic on this."

We had been discussing what I feel to be the utterly absurd Catholic doctrine that the bread and wine are literally transformed into the corporal body and blood of Jesus Christ. Now, as far as she was concerned, the matter was settled.

I then pointed out to her, in a manner that I hoped would mirror her own sweet concern, "But, dear sister, didn't you read further where Jesus said . . .

'. . . *It is the spirit that quickeneth; the flesh profiteth nothing: the words that I speak unto you, they are spirit, and they are life'* (John 6:63)?"

She was totally nonplussed, perhaps even *shocked*. She just did not know what to say. She finally asked quietly, "Is that in the Bible? I didn't know those words existed." She was so taken aback that she had little more to say.

She finally offered, somewhat flustered, the suggestion that she was not as well equipped as a priest would be to answer my reservations about the Catholic position.

I have, however, had innumerable discussions with any number of priests on just such subjects, and basically they seem to know about as much (or as little) as she does. It seems to be Catholic practice to memorize certain, specific passages that appear to support Catholic doctrines while acquiring little *general* knowledge of the Word of God.

THE MASS, HOLY COMMUNION, THE LORD'S SUPPER, THE HOLY EUCHARIST, OR THE BLESSED SACRAMENT

All of the foregoing terms are used almost interchangeably to refer to the Lord's Supper. In fact, just about all Christians observe the Lord's Supper in one form or another.

While New Testament accounts of the inception of the Lord's Supper are wonderfully simple, very little within Catholic usage remains simple for long. Under Catholic administration, it soon becomes complicated and barely recognizable as an extension of the same principles espoused within the Word of God.

To try to bring some coherence into the general subject under discussion, let us look at four areas in regard to the Roman Catholic Mass — or the Lord's Supper, if you prefer:

- The Mass as observed in Roman Catholic ritual

- The doctrine of transubstantiation

- Salvation through participation in the Mass

- What the *Bible* teaches about the Lord's Supper

THE MASS IN ROMAN CATHOLIC RITUAL

To begin with, it is (according to Catholic theology) a mortal (spiritually fatal) sin to miss Mass (without good and sufficient reason) on the Sabbath or on *holy days of obligation*. A mortal sin immediately consigns a person to hell, whatever his other spiritual condition, until it is removed by participating in *the Rite of Reconciliation —*

formerly referred to as confession, penance, absolution, and Communion.

The Roman Catholic church teaches that the Holy Mass is an expiatory (sin-removing) sacrifice, in which the Son of God actually is sacrificed anew on the cross. He literally descends into the priest's hands during the act of transubstantiation, wherein the elements of the *host* (the wafer) literally are transformed into the body, blood, soul, and divinity of our Lord Jesus Christ. This was defined as such by the Council of Trent, although minor alterations were made in wording during the Second Vatican Council.

Further, this repeated sacrifice of Christ can be specifically applied to benefit deceased souls if this is the expressed wish of living persons who donate specified sums to help defray the costs of such Masses. The Catholic church further teaches that the laity may receive full benefit of participation in the Mass by taking only the bread, while the priest alone receives both the bread and the cup.

Bartholomew F. Brewer, former Catholic priest, states:

"We are taught some incredible things about the host, the wafer that Catholics receive in Communion. Canon I, on the Most Holy Sacrament of the Eucharist, reads, 'If anyone denieth, that, in the sacrament of the most Holy Eucharist, are contained truly, really, and substantially, the body and blood together with the soul and divinity of our Lord Jesus Christ, and consequentially the whole Christ; but saith that He is only therein as in a sign, or in figure, or virtue; let him be anathema.'"

(In other words, if the person fails to believe in the doctrine of transubstantiation, he is lost.)

"We were taught," Bartholomew Brewer further states, *"that when the priest hovers over the wafer and says, 'This is my body,' it becomes the actual flesh of Christ. Likewise, after the priest says the words, 'This is*

my blood,' the wine is said to become the actual blood of Jesus. It is true that Jesus said, 'This is my body . . . this is my blood,' but it is obvious that He was speaking figuratively, just as He did when He said, **'I am the true vine, and my Father is the husbandman'** *(John 15:1).*

"This dogma about the host — sometimes called the 'wafer-God,'" Dr. Brewer goes on to state, *"has given rise to some strange doings. If, for example, the consecrated host is dropped and a mouse or other animal snatches the wafer away, the priest is given a forty-day penance to perform. If the sacramental wine is spilt at Mass, the priest is advised to lick it up and clean the place with a special cloth called a purificator. If the priest vomits after consuming the bread or the wine, it is recommended that he consume the vomit, provided that he can do it without creating an embarrassing scene. The alternative is to burn what he vomited. And such things have happened many times; I myself recall times that the Mass was being said on tossing Navy ships and the priest became seasick."*

IS THE LORD'S SUPPER A SACRAMENT OR AN ORDINANCE?

If the word "sacrament" is used to define a formal religious act used as "a symbol or memorial to a spiritual reality," it could be called a "sacrament" without doing violence to Scripture. However, if the word "sacrament" is meant to indicate a "sacrifice," wherein the Lord's death is repeated over and over again (as a formal religious act or as a sign instituted by Jesus Christ), then it should *not* be referred to as a "sacrament."

Perhaps the word "ordinance" would be more appropriate or acceptable for the New Testament Christian. This simply infers "an act of arranging something ordained or decreed by Deity, a prescribed usage, a practice, or a ceremony.'' However, it must be understood that to the Roman Catholic mind the Mass *is* a ''sacrament,'' which implies a ''sacrifice.'' This belief lies at the very heart of Catholicism.

Clark Butterfield, a former American Roman Catholic priest, who wrote about the Mass after his conversion to Christ in 1978, stated:

''[If] you . . . have never been subjected to the Roman Catholic system, [you] will always be at somewhat of a loss to fully understand and empathize with the Catholic and his 'Jesus in the Blessed Sacrament' [orientation]. You may read about it, hear about it, and study it, but its subjective reality will ultimately elude you.

''Conversely,'' Clark Butterfield went on to say, *''you who have experienced the Catholic way will recognize immediately the reality of which I write. The reality is an enigma to all outside the Catholic tradition. It is an enigma to Evangelicals because they rightfully ask, 'How can an idolatrous misconstruing of the Saviour's words and actions have aught of good in it? How can such folly be the very bedrock of the spiritual lives of countless millions of Roman Catholics?'*

''But to the Catholic, and to many former Catholics, it is the Reality, the final refuge even beyond Mary and the church itself.''

Try to comprehend this. Among the staggering number of Roman Catholics throughout the world, there will be, in God's plan, untold numbers who are earnestly searching for a personal relationship with the One they perceive to be their Redeemer.

Where can they hope to find such a personal relationship? God help us, almost without exception (and without the merciful intervention of the Holy Spirit) this will be in the figure of the *transformed host* on the altar — where the prosaic bread and wine have supposedly been changed into the living body and blood of the risen Jesus Christ.

It is said that with ex-Catholics the single most traumatic aspect of their separation from the church lies in their *new concept of Holy Communion*. With an expanded and proper grounding in Holy Scripture, they can surrender their dependence on the mediation of Mary and the saints. They can even survive without the cathartic effect of confession and penance. They eventually come to view the whole church of Jesus Christ, along with the Catholic church, in a new perspective based on scriptural concepts. But there is a longer struggle and a greater psychological dependence on the Blessed Sacrament question than on any other single element of their changed situations.

Finally, Roman Catholic doctrine says (without equivocation) that when Jesus Christ, on the night preceding His crucifixion, said, *"This is my body"* (Matthew 26:26), the bread He was holding literally became His physical body. When He took the cup and said, *"This is my blood"* (Matthew 26:28), He meant that the cup no longer contained wine, it suddenly contained His blood (which does cause some conflict with Acts 15:20 in which the New Testament church is forbidden to imbibe blood). And, when Christ added the words, *"This do in remembrance of me"* (Luke 22:19), He was actually ordaining the apostles as priests eternally to reoffer this sacrifice — or at least so says the Roman Catholic church.

This esoteric sacrifice was to be a recreation of His suffering and death on Calvary, perpetually repeated within His church until He should come again. Therefore, He is today the truly present body, blood, soul, and divinity (although, admittedly, disguised as wine and bread) on all Catholic altars and in all Catholic tabernacles, and will so remain until such time as He may choose to come again.

THE DOCTRINE OF TRANSUBSTANTIATION

The Catholic doctrine of transubstantiation is, without question, one of the most absurd doctrines ever imposed on a trusting public. As we have already discussed, this doctrine states that the priest is endowed with the power to transform bread and wine into the literal body and blood of Christ. The Roman Catholic Catechism of Christian Doctrine says:

"The Holy Mass is one and the same sacrifice with that of the Cross inasmuch as Christ, who offered Himself, a bleeding victim, on the Cross to His Heavenly Father, continues to offer Himself in the unbloody manner on the altar, through the ministry of His priests."

Roman Catholic errors are inevitably human innovations that were inserted into the church during the early centuries. This teaching on the Eucharist follows this pattern.

In the first century, as described in the New Testament, Holy Communion was a meal of fellowship eaten as a memorial to the death of Christ and a symbol of unity among Christians — both with each other and with Christ.

In the second century it began to shift toward a *ceremony*, in which Christ was present in some undefined form. This was not yet the eventual Catholic doctrine of transubstantiation — which was a development of the Middle Ages — but it was a *beginning* in this unfortunate direction.

By the third century the idea of sacrifice began to intrude, whereby Christ's body and blood were mysteriously produced by an ordained priest for the gratification and benefit of both the living and the dead.

Michael A. Smith, an English ecclesiastical historian, tells it well in his essay on the worship patterns of early Christians:

"The central service of worship on Sunday in the Early Church was the 'breaking of bread,' or 'Communion.' This was a fellowship meal, with preaching, Bible reading, and prayer, which culminated in the formal acts taken over from the Last Supper. The aim was to remember Jesus' death, and to celebrate His resurrection. Praise and thanksgiving were uppermost, and for this reason the name 'eucharist' (Greek for thanksgiving) was often given to the occasion. Gradually, the eucharist became more formal, and the meal aspect secondary.

"From the third century, Old Testament ideas of priesthood were used by some to interpret the eucharist as the 'Christian sacrifice.' At first the sacrifice was thought to consist of praises, but gradually it came to be held that an offering was made to God to gain forgiveness of sins. By the Middle Ages this had been developed to make the eucharist a re-offering of Christ's sacrifice on the cross.

"There also arose magical ideas concerning the bread and wine. By the fourth century it was held that either when the words of the Last Supper were repeated . . . or when the Holy Spirit was invoked on the bread and wine . . . a change took place. It was felt right to venerate the bread and wine as representing Jesus visibly."

This doctrine of transubstantiation, which simply means that the bread and wine change to His body and blood, was first formulated by Paschasius Radbertus, Abbot of Corbey, at the beginning of the ninth century.

It was first named transubstantiation by Hildebert of Tours in the early years of the twelfth century, and made an article of faith (official doctrine) by the Lateran Council in the beginning of the thirteenth century.

In all honesty, we must repudiate this dogma on two counts:

• It is opposed to Scripture.

- It is contradicted by the evidence of the senses. When a person handles the wine or the wafer, the textures remain the same. They taste the same. There is no transformation in odor. They are still bread and juice, with all the original qualities. They are physically unchanged and will ever remain unchanged. They are merely, as blessed and holy as they might be, a memorial to our Saviour's sacrifice as a sin offering in our stead.

Therefore, we reject this erroneous doctrine because of its basically superstitious nature and the idolatrous connotations connected with it.

A thoughtful study of Paul's epistle to the Hebrews should lead us at least to *question* the Roman doctrine of the continuing sacrifice of the Mass. Please note these verses:

> *"For such an high priest became us, who is holy, harmless, undefiled, separate from sinners, and made higher than the heavens; Who needeth not daily, as those high priests, to offer up sacrifice, first for his own sins, and then for the people's: for this he did once, when he offered up himself"* (Hebrews 7:26, 27).

> *"But Christ being come an high priest of good things to come, by a greater and more perfect tabernacle, not made with hands, that is to say, not of this building; Neither by the blood of goats and calves, but by his own blood he entered in once into the holy place, having obtained eternal redemption for us"* (Hebrews 9:11, 12).

> *"For Christ is not entered into the holy places made with hands, which are the figures of the true; but into heaven itself, now to appear in the presence of God for us: Nor yet that he should offer himself often, as the high priest entereth into the holy place every year with blood of others; For then must he often have suffered since the foundation of the world: but now once in the end of the world hath he appeared to put away sin by the sacrifice of himself"* (Hebrews 9:24-26).

These verses confirm the "once-and-for-all" character of Christ's sacrifice. Obviously, this allows for no repetition. So the clear teaching of God's Word expressly contradicts any continuing sacrifice — after the manner of the Catholic Mass.

The Bible teaching is clear and concise. Any future sacrifices were repudiated when Jesus paid the price for all future sin and cried out, *"It is finished"* (John 19:30).

Actually, the phrase uttered by Jesus (in the Greek, *teleo*) was a colloquial expression that meant "paid in full" or "the debt is cleared forever."

So, how might a person explain this cleavage between New Testament teaching and Catholic dogma? Of course, we know that scriptural error invariably stems from the evil one, Satan. In this case it was due, at least in part, to dabblings into the popular Eastern mystery religions, borrowing from Greek and Roman paganism and reverting to outmoded, Old Testament, Mosaic customs — all of which demanded recurring sacrificial offerings.

It is just one more tragic example of what happens when man's misguided intellect strays from the written Word of God.

The Catholic doctrine of transubstantiation forces a person to humiliate Christ, even beyond the supreme humiliation He suffered on the cross at Calvary. The glorified, risen, and ascended Christ can never again be degraded by any force, human or spiritual. Yet the very concept of bread and wine, which He Himself created — being mysteriously transformed into His living body and blood — forces Him into further humiliation, which is unacceptable and unthinkable.

SALVATION THROUGH THE MASS

To the Roman Catholic mind, the blessed sacrament (the Mass) is a critical element in his salvation (going to heaven).

The Mass is the Catholic means of worshiping Jesus. Whatever the degree of involvement with Catholicism, the Catholic never trifles with the awesome concept of the Eucharist, or Blessed Sacrament, being Jesus. However misdirected he may be in his daily life, when it comes time to confront that Presence, he renounces all vices until he has received Jesus at Holy Communion.

As a logical extension of the doctrine of transubstantiation, it has also become dogma that consecrated bread and wine should be publicly and privately adored and venerated. As a result, the Roman Catholic church has adopted a number of rituals (in the form of various feasts and devotions) to promote adoration and veneration of these physical elements that have been *transformed* into the Godhead. The principal feast is Holy Thursday, or the Feast of Corpus Christi (Latin for "the body of Christ"). The principal devotions are Benediction of the Blessed Sacrament, Forty Hours Devotions, and Perpetual Adoration of the Sacrament (in certain designated churches). Each feast has its own particular rites and each devotion its individual ceremonies or customs.

At Mass the priest consecrates — in addition to the bread and wine he will consume during the Mass — the hosts to be received by the faithful at the Mass. (Because of the alcoholism problem among priests, the Vatican now allows common grape juice to be substituted by alcoholic priests.)

Each wafer is called a host. There are small hosts for the congregation and a large host for the priest. Moreover, the priest may consecrate additional small hosts to be retained in a chalice held within the tabernacle between Masses. Furthermore, he may consecrate an additional large host, also to be reserved in the tabernacle, but to be used later for public display and adoration. (As previously noted, nothing is ever simple within the rites of Roman Catholicism.)

So there is, almost always — in every Catholic church — some consecrated bread reserved in the tabernacle, which means that Jesus is physically present within the church — although firmly locked within the interior of the tabernacle. This is the reason Catholics genuflect (touch their knee to the ground) as they enter and leave their churches — even when no service is in progress. It is also the reason Catholics maintain a somber silence in their churches and why candles burn perpetually in the sanctuary. Jesus is present, in the tabernacle, although in the form of bread. (The tabernacle, usually an ornate and expensive vault that maintains the security of the expensive chalices holding the hosts, represents the central focus of the church arrangement and occupies a central position over the altar.)

Although the hosts stored within the tabernacle are not usually visible to the public, parishioners are encouraged to come to the church at almost any hour to pray, to adore, and to be comforted by the consecrated hosts.

INDULGENCES

Numerous indulgences are granted to Catholics who observe this custom. (An indulgence is a reduction in the sentences imposed on Catholics [in purgatory] where past sins [which have been forgiven through confession and penance] are personally atoned for by torment imposed by God.)

In effect, the granting of indulgences suggests that the church issues (and God affirms) these reductions in sentence.

Indulgences can be either saved up for personal use after death by the person earning the indulgence or cashed in immediately by crediting them to the account of loved ones who already have died. As no one knows precisely how long sentences in purgatory run (perhaps for centuries), it is obviously prudent to save up as many indulgences as possible.

This Roman teaching (of purgatory and indulgences) blatantly ignores the fact that Jesus Christ accepted *all* the guilt for our sins. It further ignores God's statement:

> *"And their sins and iniquities will I remember no more"* (Hebrews 10:17).

It was scandals over the selling of indulgences that first inflamed Martin Luther against excesses within the church, and indirectly brought about the Protestant Reformation.

One former priest states that he made innumerable visits to countless cathedrals in Europe and in numerous local churches — where he would spend long hours kneeling in solitary prayer and adoration before tabernacles —

venerating the consecrated bits of bread. Basically, he went on to say, this was the only time he ever felt really close to Jesus Christ. And then he added the solemn truth that "feeling close" to Christ is a far cry from trusting Him for salvation.

In addition to private and personal adoration of the Blessed Sacrament, ornate and ostentatious public ceremonies are calculated to promote fervid devotion to the Eucharist. On such occasions the larger host is brought out from behind the altar and inserted in a glass-fronted receptacle within a monstrance.

The monstrance is a portable, ornate, and expensive device of precious metals (and sometimes jewels), which is shaped vaguely like a cross but with a prominent sunburst effect around the area where the host is displayed.

Because of the glass front, a person can actually see Jesus (or the host) as it is transported about the premises by a priest.

The monstrance routinely is paraded through churches during Benediction (usually after the last Mass on Sunday morning), during which a ceremony of sprinkling holy water and shaking vessels of incense accompanies the Lord's trip around the church. The monstrance is also the vehicle for transporting the host for veneration during many festivals in Latin American countries.

And such is the average worshiper's relationship with the Jesus of the Eucharist. Clark Butterfield said it was a love-fear relationship: love because he was told it was Jesus, fear because he was terrified that he might dishonor the sacrament through some carelessness, and continuing apprehension that he might at some time receive the sacrament unworthily in Communion.

To the convicted Catholic, transubstantiation means that the bread and wine no longer remain; they have actually become the body and blood of Christ.

In addition, during the Mass, a true sacrifice is constituted when the priest pronounces the words of consecration. Calvary is renewed, restored, and replayed before the eyes of the assembled congregation. A person is physically there at the foot of the cross as Jesus serves as propitiation for his sins.

In Roman Catholicism the Eucharist is central to all worship. It is an integral part of salvation. What it amounts to is that this is the basic Catholic relationship with Jesus Christ.

THE QUESTION MUST BE ASKED: IS THIS IDOLATRY?

The Catholic Catechism (the basic guidebook on Catholic doctrine) defines "idolatry" as "rendering to any creature the honor and adoration that are due to God alone." I think a person would have to agree that what we have described in the preceding pages constitutes idolatry — the worshiping of a piece of bread that a person has become convinced is the Lord Jesus Christ.

WHAT DOES THE BIBLE TEACH ABOUT THE LORD'S SUPPER?

Luke, the beloved physician, said:

> *"And he took bread, and gave thanks, and brake it, and gave unto them, saying, This is my body which is given for you: this do in remembrance of me. Likewise also the cup after supper, saying, This cup is the new testament in my blood, which is shed for you"* (Luke 22:19).

Mark, the evangelist, said:

"And they all drank of it" (Mark 14:23).

(It is interesting that the Lord never used the word "wine." The word "cup" is used instead.)

The Apostle Paul said:

"For as often as ye eat this bread, and drink this cup, ye do shew the Lord's death till he come. Wherefore whosoever shall eat this bread, and drink this cup of the Lord, unworthily, shall be guilty of the body and blood of the Lord. But let a man examine himself, and so let him eat of that bread, and drink of that cup. For he that eateth and drinketh unworthily, eateth and drinketh damnation to himself, not discerning the Lord's body" (I Corinthians 11:26-29).

It is sad but true that tens (and even hundreds) of millions of Catholics drink the cup of the Lord unworthily — guilty of the body and blood of the Lord — simply because they do not rightfully discern the Lord's body.

They think the host and the wine actually become His personal flesh and blood, so they worship bread — which constitutes a form of idolatry. They do not understand what the Lord said, respecting the sacrifice He would shortly offer at Calvary.

The words, *"This is my body . . . this is my blood"* (Matthew 26:26, 28), are accepted literally in Catholic dogma. On the same basis we should accept without thinking that Jesus gives us literal living waters, which will produce eternal life (John 4:14), or that Jesus is truly a door (John 10:7-9), that He is a lamb (John 1:29), or that He is a growing vine (John 15:5).

If the Catholic hierarchy is to be consistent, they *should* foster adoration of doors, vines, and lambs. Certainly, these figures of speech are descriptive and colorful, but they are transparently figurative, just as are the terms *"my body"* and *"my blood."* The New Testament church and the Early Church understood and accepted this just as it was offered — *as a figure of speech.*

In Catholic theology much is made of the sixth chapter of the Gospel of John (which we have already mentioned), which recounts the discourse of Jesus in which He referred to Himself as *". . . the living bread which came down from heaven"* (John 6:51).

Catholic doctrine states that Jesus was here depicting Himself as the Eucharist — to be literally consumed as a means to eternal life.

However, at the end of this discourse Jesus demolished any such carnal interpretation by adding:

> *"Doth this offend you? . . . It is the spirit that quickeneth; the flesh profiteth nothing: the words that I speak unto you, they are spirit, and they are life"* (John 6:61-63).

So how *do* we "eat and drink" of His flesh and blood? By *coming* to Him to end our spiritual hunger, and by *believing* in Him to end our spiritual thirst. This does *not* come by eating some magically transformed bread and by drinking some magically changed wine.

But, insists the Roman Catholic, "Why did Christ use the words *'hoc est corpum meum'*? Why did He not say, 'This is a *symbol* of my body'?"

For all intents and purposes, this is an excellent question. But we must remember that when the Lord initiated this holy memorial to His death, He was eating the *Passover* feast with His disciples. Passover was established centuries before as a memorial for Israel of the awesome event that had taken place while they were in bondage in Egypt. The firstborn of every family then residing in Egypt would be slain, *except* those who had established their faith in God by trusting in the blood placed on their doorposts as a sign that their house should be exempt.

Now, however, the Passover was to be abandoned as a memorial to the saving grace of God Almighty, and a *new* memorial created — to the ultimate salvation that had only been *foretold* by the original Passover. In effect, *the Lord's Supper was to be the Christian replacement for the Hebrew Passover.*

From that moment on the Christian community (God's new Israel) would be able to celebrate a *greater* liberation than that from Egyptian slavery. Finally, man was to be freed from the bondage of sin and condemnation through the sacrifice of ". . . *the Lamb of God, which taketh away the sin of the world*" (John 1:29).

When the Israelites partook of the Passover meal, no one was confused. No one believed that the lamb they were eating was the true body of the Lord's Passover. They were fully aware that it was only a *representation*, a *memorial*, of the event they were commemorating.

In view of this, it is perfectly clear why the Lord should employ, for the new commemoration, words that reflected the rites of the old. Nor did He doubt that the common sense of the disciples would enable them to understand that this was a figurative and not a literal statement.

It is clear to anyone who has studied the New Testament that this *is* the manner in which the apostles interpreted it. This is confirmed by the fact that their standard reference to this act was simply that of *breaking bread*.

"And they continued stedfastly in the apostles' doctrine and fellowship, and in breaking of

> *bread, and in prayers . . . and many wonders*
> *and signs were done by the apostles . . . . And,*
> *they continuing daily with one accord in the*
> *temple, and breaking bread from house to*
> *house, did eat their meat with gladness and*
> *singleness of heart, Praising God, and having*
> *favour with all the people. And the Lord added*
> *to the church daily such as should be saved"*
> (Acts 2:42-47; compare Acts 20:7).

> *"The cup of blessing which we bless, is it not*
> *the communion of the blood of Christ? The*
> *bread which we break, is it not the communion*
> *of the body of Christ?"* (I Corinthians 10:16).

No Roman Catholic would refer to the Holy Mass as "breaking bread" without adding complicated explanations. Yet, in the New Testament the Apostle Paul twice referred to the Lord's admonition, *"This do in remembrance of me"* (Luke 22:19; compare I Corinthians 11:24, 25).

Paul then added (in the form of a comment):

> *"For as often as ye eat this bread, and drink*
> *this cup, ye do shew the Lord's death till he*
> *come"* (I Corinthians 11:26).

Please note several things. He did not say, "Ye shall eat His *body* and drink His *blood*." He referred to the ritual as employing bread and a cup. If these were legitimately the blood and body of Christ, Paul would certainly have referred to them as such.

Further, Paul did *not* say, "Ye shall *repeat the sacrifice of Christ* until He comes." He said, *"Ye do shew the Lord's death."* The Greek word here translated "shew" is *kataggello*, which means "to declare, preach, speak, or teach." It does *not* mean to reenact or reproduce. Also, the words *"drink this cup"* are plural, which suggests that, at least in the Corinthian church, *all* partook of the cup — not just one individual, the priest, as in the Catholic Mass.

A COMMEMORATION — NOT A SACRIFICE

That the Communion should be a *re*-offering of the very body of Christ to humiliation and sacrifice, or as it is called within Catholic usage, a repetition of the sacrifice, is an idea that is obviously variant with *many* passages of sacred Scripture. For example:

> *"If they shall fall away, to renew them again unto repentance; seeing they crucify to themselves the Son of God afresh, and put him to an open shame"* (Hebrews 6:6).

These all assure us that the death of Christ was a *unique* act, and one that would be sufficient for the remission of *all* sins for *all* time.

It seems obvious that if the expiatory death of Jesus was a perfect work, we have no need for additional sacrifices. There should be no further need for even "bloodless" sacrifices to finish any work of redemption.

> *"The blood of Jesus Christ his Son cleanseth us from all sin"* (I John 1:7).

If the celebration of the Mass were a *true* sacrifice, it would be wicked and cruel for the priests to repeat it so frequently. If, as argued, this is a *mystic* sacrifice (rather than a real one) and the Son of God does not really suffer (as He did on Calvary), then why refer to it *as* a sacrifice? No true sacrifice exists without pain and suffering.

That the celebration of the Eucharist by the Roman Catholic church is labeled a "sacrifice," rather than a "commemoration," is due partly to the pagan custom of calling everything offered to the gods a sacrifice.

The New Testament clearly shows that the Lord's Supper was only a *peripheral* element in the overall majesty of the Gospel message. It was obviously not considered an essential part of salvation. There is no hint anywhere within God's Word that the edible elements involved with the Last Supper were ever adored (or *meant* to be adored) by Christians.

To be sure, the rite was commanded by the Lord. He did say, *"This do."* But to put everything into focus, He also said, *". . . in remembrance of me"* (Luke 22:19).

So we do exactly that.

We partake of the Holy Communion in remembrance of the Lord Jesus Christ. We recall and remember, and always will, that His body was given as a perfect sin offering and that His blood was shed for each and every one of us.

WE CLOSE WITH THE WORD OF GOD

"Who hath believed our report? and to whom is the arm of the Lord revealed? For he shall grow up before him as a tender plant, and as a root out of a dry ground: he hath no form nor comeliness; and when we shall see him, there is no beauty that we should desire him. He is despised and rejected of men; a man of sorrows, and acquainted with grief: and we hid as it were our faces from him; he was despised, and we esteemed him not. Surely he hath borne our

griefs, and carried our sorrows: yet we did esteem him stricken, smitten of God, and afflicted. But he was wounded for our transgressions, he was bruised for our iniquities: the chastisement of our peace was upon him; and with his stripes we are healed. All we like sheep have gone astray; we have turned every one to his own way; and the Lord hath laid on him the iniquity of us all. He was oppressed, and he was afflicted, yet he opened not his mouth: he is brought as a lamb to the slaughter, and as a sheep before her shearers is dumb, so he openeth not his mouth . . . . Therefore will I divide him a portion with the great, and he shall divide the spoil with the strong; because he hath poured out his soul unto death: and he was numbered with the transgressors; and he bare the sin of many, and made intercession for the transgressors" (Isaiah 53:1-7, 12).

CHAPTER
FIVE

THE
CATHOLIC
CONFESSIONAL

lark Butterfield, former Catholic priest, made a statement in his book, *Night Journey From Rome to the New Jerusalem*. In describing a funeral he attended in a Catholic church *after* having left the Catholic priesthood, Butterfield related:

"Then we entered the nave of the church. The muted light danced with subdued colors from the stained glass windows, even on that dull winter morning. Scores of pious statues loomed darkly about the sanctuary and the side altars at the far end of the aisle. Red and blue vigil lights flickered in separate locations before garish images of the Lord, the Virgin, and the saints.

"Then I shifted my gaze to the side walls of the back of the nave. There were situated some of the confessional cubicles. In an instant the old revulsion, the fear, the hatred, and the despair washed over me! I felt the buffeting of Satan.

"'Let's get out of here; it's too hot,' I whispered to Steve. Good, simple Steve did not ask for an explanation. We donned our coats and stepped out the front door into the February cold. A few cars were now pulling up in the hard-packed snow, discharging mourners at the church steps. I reminded myself, to end the turmoil, 'I am saved by the blood of Christ; I am loved by Him. The bondage of the Roman Sacrament of Penance has no power to wound my spirit.'"

The Catholic believer is taught early that penance is one of the "seven sacraments instituted by Christ for the salvation of men."

WORDS OF THE CONFESSIONAL

Catholic dogma states unequivocally that Jesus gave His apostles the specific power to forgive or retain sins and that this power has resided within the church from that day to this. Priests *still* have this power to forgive or retain sins, but for them to exercise this power, sinners *must confess to them verbally*. The priest then imposes a penance to be performed and grants absolution (remission of the sin) — with the understanding that the penance *must* be completed.

Until recently the ritual for absolution included recitation of these precise words:

"May Our Lord Jesus Christ absolve you, and by His authority I absolve you from your sins, in the name of the Father, and of the Son, and of the Holy Spirit."

Further, the church of Rome teaches that each Catholic *must* confess his sins to a priest at least once a year, preferably during Lent. This is known as "the Easter duty" and is essential not only for salvation, but for membership in good standing in the Catholic church.

Annual confession is only a *minimum* standard for membership. Weekly (or even more frequent) confession is considered closer to the ideal.

ORIGINS OF THE CONFESSIONAL

This doctrine of confession is neatly and logically presented within the Catechism and in official church histories. But its *actual* history as an accepted element within the Catholic structure is far less clear-cut and rational. Even Catholic historians and theologians within the organized hierarchy are hard pressed to produce a convincing background for this practice of auricular (verbal) confession.

It is frustrating to attempt *accurately* to trace the story of its introduction, its spread, and its final imposition as a prerequisite to the forgiveness of sins. The story entails uncertainties, historical absurdities, hierarchical scheming, and theological revisionism.

So if auricular confession was *not* established by Jesus Christ — nor practiced by the apostles — where did Rome acquire this custom that was to become a basic building block of the Catholic faith? There can be little doubt that it came from the same source from which the Catholic church acquired a number of *additional* practices which do not agree with Scripture (as discussed in other chapters).

THIS UNSAVORY SOURCE IS EARLY PAGAN RELIGIONS

Eusibias Salvarte, the Orientalist, refers to auricular confession as an integral part of Greek rites, which quite clearly demonstrates that they came from Babylonian origin. He says:

"All the Greeks, from Delphi to Thermopylae, were initiated in the mysteries of the Temple of Delphi. Their silence in not revealing anything shows that they were enjoined to silence which was assured — not only by the penalties that were threatened should the mysteries be revealed — but also by the general confession required of the aspirants before being initiated. In this confession there was greater motive to fear the indiscreet priest than the indiscretion of the initiate.."

Dupius, in his work, *De Tous Le Sulte*, says:

"There were certain priests, called Koes, whose task was to receive the confessions and judge the faults of the penitents."

It is not unusual for Christian converts, coming from heathenism, obstinately to adhere to certain rituals and practices. Many found direct, personal confession to God unsatisfying, even though it was prescribed as such in the Holy Bible and confirmed by the most saintly men of the age. However, because of the inconvenience and embarrassment of *public* confession, private confession to a priest, it seems, was a logical and desirable compromise.

In the beginning this amounted more to a confession to God with the priest *participating* by suggesting the penance, rather than an overt confession to the priest. At this point the priest did not forgive the sin, he merely guided the meeting between the penitent and God.

EVOLUTION OF THE DOGMA OF CONFESSION

OPTIONAL

For many centuries confession was *optional* as a means of receiving counsel from a priest and of resolving the pangs of a person's conscience through the doing of some penance (which, of course, the priest would suggest). Many penitents continued in the traditional (and prescribed) manner of confessing their sins directly to God.

PUBLIC

We find in the history of the church that from the second through the fifth centuries, confession of sins (after having first been made directly to God) was practiced from time to time before the whole congregation as a demonstration of public repentance. Such public confessions could, of course, have grave consequences, depending on the nature of the sins.

PENITENTIARY PRESBYTERS

To avoid this, the first experiment in auricular confession was begun at Constantinople in A.D. 329 with the creation of "penitentiary presbyters." These were a special class of priests intended to hear confessions, and to declare whether they were convenient (and prudent) to confess in public.

But in A.D. 390 the office of penitentiary presbyters was abolished by Bishop Nestorius — due to a scandal involving one of the presbyters and a woman penitent.

In his pastoral letter abolishing the office, Nestorius stated that in the future *"each person will be left in liberty to participate or not in the holy mystery of the communion, according to his conscience."*

Now this begs a question.

If auricular confession had been practiced by all the ministers of the Gospel since apostolic times (as the Catholic church states) why would there have been a need to create the penitentiary presbyters? Even more puzzling, did this mean Nestorius was abolishing the power of the priest to to forgive sins which Jesus had established among the apostles?

It was only very slowly, and as the priests gained influence, that it become more common to substitute confession to the priest for direct, personal confession to God.

However, even with all this backward, forward, and lateral movement taking place, *it would be a thousand years before a priest would assume the responsibility of personally pardoning sins.* Up until then the penitent was dismissed after his confession with a simple and fitting phrase: "May God forgive you and take away your sin."

MODERN ABSOLUTION

The modern form of absolution, *"Ego te absolve"* ("I forgive you"), considered to be *essential* to the sacrament today, cannot be found in any authenticated document throughout the first twelve centuries of the Christian era. During this period the absolution formula employed by the Roman church was, *"Ablutio criminum, Misereatur tui omnipotens Deus, et dimittat tibi omnia pecatta tua"* ("May God omnipotent give you absolution and forgive you").

Thomas Aquinas, philosopher and scholar who lived in the thirteenth century (*about* A.D. 1224-1274), inadvertently revealed the date of this important change from the traditional to the modern ritual. This respected writer and doctor of theology mentioned that a contemporary was complaining against the *authoritarian* form of absolution (where the priest takes the authority). In discussing this matter, he mentioned that it had been only thirty years since the professors had used the *supplicatory* (traditional, quoted above) form. *So, we know that it was about*

A.D. 1200 that priests first assumed the authority to personally *forgive sin*.

OBLIGATORY

This important development was introduced, it seems, at the same time as the edict that made confession *obligatory* for all members of the church. This was at the Fourth Lateran Council, celebrated in A.D. 1215), where annual, auricular confession became mandatory for all persons who had reached the age of reason, on pain of mortal sin — which meant that eternal damnation was the penalty for ignoring this order.

In other words, even though a person had not sinned during the year, he would still be consigned to eternal hellfire — simply because he had not "reported in" to the priest during the year.

Claude Fleury, French ecclesiastical historian (A.D. 1640-1723), states:

"This is the first canon I know of that commands general confession."

From this Fourth Lateran Council on, it has been the duty of every Roman Catholic to confess his sins to a priest to receive not only counsel but also absolution. *This is, of course, contrary to the teaching and example of the New Testament.*

PERILS OF THE CONFESSIONAL

PROMISCUITY ENCOURAGED

The first thing that should be noted about the Roman Catholic confessional is that *it is contrary to good morals.*
Why?

Because it encourages promiscuity in behavior by providing a simple and mechanical format for putting a person's sinful behavior behind him. The thought that any transgression can be undone by observing a quick and simple ritual, thus blotting out the pangs of conscience, makes future forays off the beaten path all that much more attractive. After *repeated* excursions into the realm of sin, with quick absolution each time, the practitioner soon becomes inured to the momentary tremors of conscience. *"Why not? I'll just go to confession tomorrow."*

Now, please understand. We are not minimizing the fact that the counsel and advice given by many Catholic priests can provide consolation and guidance to those coming for confession. But we maintain that this same ministry *could* be provided *outside* the confessional — in an environment relieved of the mechanical and dehumanizing aspects of a ritual, and of the time pressures imposed by a waiting line of impatient parishioners. They could further be provided without the incidental and baseless contention that the priest will "broker" God's forgiveness. The remorseful Catholic *could* be directed to a personal audience with God for the dissolution of the sin element, and *then* the priest could offer ministry for the personal problems besetting the disturbed layman.

PRIESTLY DEFECTS

Every human priest has several great (and human) defects in exercising the office of confessor:

- The priest does not know the spiritual condition of the sinner, so he cannot be sure whether the person's repentance is genuine or not. Only God knows the secrets of the heart (Psalm 44:21).

- The priest knows even less of the *thoughts* of God. He can in no way ascertain whether God has, in fact, pardoned the supposed penitent, to whom he is almost *obligated* (by the very nature of the ritual) to provide his *"Ego te absolve."* Thus his words may or may *not* conform to the truth — engendering in the person receiving absolution a false sense of security.

- No mortal man can forgive sin. Jesus said:

> *"Whose soever sins ye remit, they are remitted unto them; and whose soever sins ye retain, they are retained"* (John 20:23).

Of course, this is the Scripture the Catholic church uses as authority for their priests' ability to forgive sins. *However,* the *original* Greek should be studied. Here the words translated "remitted" and "retained" are in the perfect tense. This indicates an action *already* performed. So the Greek more accurately would be translated as, "If you forgive the sins of any, they have already been forgiven. If you retain the sins of any, they have already been retained."

The interpretation of the Catholic church reverses the order given in the original, saying instead (of the priest), *"You* can forgive sins and then your decision *will* be approved in heaven."

But Scripture says, in essence, "Your sins have already been forgiven in heaven, through acceptance of your proclamation of forgiveness through the blood of Jesus Christ."

This means, in effect, that any disciple (for Jesus addressed *all* present when He made this statement, not just the apostles) can assure any sinner that his sins have been forgiven the moment he comes to Christ in repentant faith. Likewise, the disciple (and the Christian who trusts Jesus for salvation) can assure any *non*believer that his sins are retained *unless* he trusts in Christ for his salvation.

THE APOSTLES DID NOT HAVE
THE POWER TO FORGIVE SINS

The remainder of the New Testament bears out the intent of this passage. Furthermore, every major doctrine within the Word of God appears more than once, as self-confirmation. For example:

> *"That in the mouth of two or three witnesses every word may be established"* (Matthew 18:16).

But there is no other statement in the Bible that even *suggests* that anyone can forgive sin but God. There is no incident where a disciple or apostle forgives sins by his own authority.

Did the Apostle Peter give absolution to Cornelius (Acts 10)?

Did the Apostle Paul give absolution to the Philippian jailer (Acts 16)?

No. The apostles preached salvation to their hearers and *led* them to the opportunity to receive forgiveness through the blood of Jesus Christ.

Only in this sense are there any recorded incidents of forgiveness through the actions of the apostles. *In no situation do we find the apostles calling for a personal confession to them — followed by absolution.* This would be in total opposition to the New Testament proclamation of forgiveness through repentance and acceptance of the propitiatory sacrifice of Christ at Calvary.

Peter confirmed this emphatically when he said:

"To him give all the prophets witness, that through his name whosoever believeth in him shall receive remission of sins" (Acts 10:43).

God has never given any person the authority to make a decision as to whether to forgive or retain another person's sins. Again, we must recall that the only mediator between God and man is Christ Jesus.

"For there is one God, and one mediator between God and man, the man Christ Jesus" (I Timothy 2:5).

SOME TERRIBLE DANGERS

Not only does the confessional offer an easy way of becoming absolved of sin, but it also offers to the priest — an unmarried man — the most intimate thoughts of the opposite sex. He is the recipient of revelations of conjugal intimacies (proper and improper) and the most secret thoughts a wife may have regarding her husband. Every kind of sin is confessed to him, *and it is no wonder that such revelations have produced terrible scandals — and will go on doing so until the abandonment of this danger- ous human institution.*

How many priests have been started down the road to moral degradation by listening to confessions that open the door to their involvement? The confessional is a direct contradiction of the petition Jesus Himself said we should pray:

"Lead us not into temptation" (Matthew 6:13).

How many political figures, public servants, judges, and men of high and important positions are held in bondage because of intimate secrets revealed to their priests? The most personal facts of every Catholic family, of every Catholic heart (which should be known only to God) are known by priests in their most intimate details.

How many potential scandals within the Catholic church have been *hushed up*, and how many shameful situations concerning priests have been *swept under the carpet* by politicians and public servants — just because too many secrets are known to the priest?

It has been widely publicized that J. Edgar Hoover was politically untouchable because of his "little black book," which contained intimate facts about all the political powers who might attempt to exert influence over him. If such intimate knowledge could make an individual "above the law," is it unreasonable to assume that similar knowledge could serve to make the Catholic church untouchable too?

One of the most powerful forms of bondage known to man can be the bondage of the confessional, where individuals can become the servants of priests because of revelations that become the property of the church through the confessional.

TRUE CONFESSION ACCORDING TO THE WORD OF GOD

"But thou, when thou prayest, enter into thy closet, and when thou hast shut thy door, pray to thy Father which is in secret; and thy Father which seeth in secret shall reward thee openly" (Matthew 6:6).

*"For this shall every one that is godly pray
unto thee in a time when thou mayest be found"*
(Psalm 32:6).

In the book of Acts and in all the apostolic letters, we do not find a single case where auricular confession takes place or is encouraged. Quite the contrary, one specific incident graphically illustrates the opposite: Simon the Sorcerer (Acts 8:9-24) offered the apostles money if they would reveal to him the secret of receiving the baptism in the Holy Spirit. Peter upbraided him for thinking that the gift of God could be obtained for money and then told him:

*"Pray God, if perhaps the thought of thine
heart may be forgiven thee"* (Acts 8:22).

Note that Peter did *not* say, "Confess your sin to me or to some other apostle and we will give you absolution." He told him to pray to *God* for forgiveness.

It would seem that this one short passage demonstrates convincingly that the Roman contention about priests forgiving sins is *not* harmonious with what the Word of God says about forgiveness.

ANOTHER KIND OF PARDON

In the New Testament we have an interesting example of a kind of pardon that has nothing to do with *divine* pardon for salvation of the soul. And even here reconciliation was not bestowed by any one person, but was granted by the group action of an entire community of believers.

One of the members of the church at Corinth had fallen into sin. The Christians of that church, meeting together in special session, had declared that the member was unworthy to partake of communion and had separated him from the fellowship of the church. The offending member then acknowledged his faults and the apostle recommended charity toward him, saying:

> *"To whom ye forgive any thing, I forgive also"* (II Corinthians 2:10).

The words *"to whom ye forgive any thing"* clearly indicate that granting of pardon is not the exclusive office of any one person, but is the responsibility of the *entire assembly*. Neither the apostle nor any other minister of the church at Corinth took on himself the individual authority to forgive. Even in this problem (involving fellowship rather than salvation), the church as a whole had to make the decision and declare the repentant brother acceptable again to their body (fellowship of believers, or the church).

THE TEACHING OF THE EARLY CHURCH FATHERS

John Chrysostom, the great preacher of the fourth century (aptly named "Golden Mouth"), wrote in one of his sermons:

"It is not necessary that anyone should witness your confession. Recognize your iniquities and let God alone, without anyone knowing, hear your confession. I exhort and entreat you to confess your sins to God. I do not tell you to reveal them to men, God alone sees your confession.

"Confess your sins daily in your prayers . . . who can doubt to make us act this way? I do not urge you to go and confess your sins to a man who is a sinner like yourselves, who might despise you if you were to relate to him your faults. But confess them to God who is able to forgive them."

Basil, bishop of Caesarea (A.D. 329-379), said:

"I do not make myself a spectacle before the world to confess with my mouth; I shut my eyes and make my confession in the privacy of my heart. Only before Thee, oh, my God, do I allow my sins to escape. Thou alone art their witness."

Augustine, bishop of Hippo (A.D. 354-430) and a great writer of apologetic and dogmatic works, declared:

"Why should I go to expose the wounds of my soul before men? It is the Holy Spirit who remits sins; man is unable to do so for he stands in the same need or in the same position as he who comes to him for the remedy."

TRUE CONFESSION

So without the confessional and absolution, how *does* the Christian find release from the sins that attack his conscience? Every time the Christian realizes he has offended God, another person, or even himself (however unintentionally), he goes personally before God in private prayer, asking for pardon and for the strength to live a more genuine Christian life. We should all seek a life that honors the profession of faith we made in our beloved Saviour (1 John 1:9).

Such a Christian cannot sin casually in the expectation that he will find a lenient confessor ready to give an easy *"Ego te absolve"* and a quick penance. *In confessing directly to God, there is no possibility of "shopping" from one priest to another in the hope of finding one who has a philosophy of behavior similar to one's own.* In true Christian confession — to God directly — there is no room for fraud, pretensions, or expectation of gullible acceptance of pleas of remorse — when we may not be feeling it. God *knows* the heart.

I believe that the superior morality found in Protestant nations (which even non-fanatical Catholics will admit exists) *is not so much a matter of culture or innate racial virtues as it is the question of the confessional.* This is crucially important in defining the moral atmosphere of any nation where the majority of the population accepts Catholic doctrine.

True Christian confession might, on the surface, appear to be easier than Roman Catholic confession. But it is actually *more* severe within the intimate realm of the spirit — which is, after all, what really matters when we discuss spiritual growth and eternal salvation, is it not?

In cases of grave and flagrant sin, true Christian churches demand a manifest proof, in *addition* to confession to God. This was mentioned earlier in reference to Paul's second letter to the church at Corinth. If the individual's repentance is genuine, the proof of which may consist of a certain period of true Christian living, he can then be readmitted to the fellowship and communion of the church (the body of Christ). No technical penance is required. The only penance required by God is *repentance.*

> *"For thou desirest not sacrifice; else would I give it: thou delightest not in burnt offering. The sacrifices of God are 'a broken spirit: a broken and a contrite heart"* (Psalm 51:16, 17).

IN CONCLUSION

And so, we find that the Catholic confessional is *not* scriptural. We find that it has its origins in heathenistic, pagan rituals. We also note that the perils of the confessional are immorality among the priesthood, the creation of a false sense of security for the penitent, and the creation of a fertile field for promiscuous behavior. It also places great numbers of individuals under bondage because the innermost secrets of the heart are bared to a priest. Such information *can* constitute a threat of moral extortion for such individuals.

We also find that true, scripturally founded confession must be made to God, and to God alone. He alone can forgive. He *will* forgive. Why, therefore, look elsewhere for false and confusing avenues to forgiveness?

CHAPTER
SIX

MARY, THE MOTHER OF GOD?

he Catholic people pray to Mary, as mediatrix:
"*Hail, Mary, full of grace, the Lord is with thee. Blessed art thou among women and blessed is the fruit of thy womb, Jesus. Holy Mary, mother of God, pray for us sinners, now and at the hour of our death. Amen.*"

A former Catholic priest wrote:

"*I can personally testify to the fact that the Jesus Christ I knew, loved, and served as a Roman Catholic is not the same Jesus Christ I know, love, and serve today. The Jesus I once knew was a wafer of bread and a cup of wine — and He had a mother called Mary who stood between Him and me. I couldn't get through to Him except through her, and He couldn't get through to me except through her.*

"*In other words, my religion back then was tantamount to — let's say — Buddhism or the Muslim religion.*

There was no difference, objectively speaking, between me as a Catholic priest, and a Moslem priest, for example."

These are some of the saddest words I have ever read. Still, they describe the situation so dramatically. How many times do I see bumper stickers that say: "CAN'T FIND JESUS? LOOK FOR HIS MOTHER."

Mary dominates every aspect of Catholic religious life. Unfortunately, this is the opposite of *biblical* Christianity.

In this chapter, I want to look at Mary as the Catholic sees her, Mary as the mediator between Jesus Christ and man, and Mary as the Bible describes her.

MARY — AS THE CATHOLIC SEES HER

"Oh, Mary, my Queen and my Mother, I give myself entirely to thee. And to show my devotion to thee, I consecrate to thee this day my eyes, my ears, my mouth, my heart, my whole being without reserve. Wherefore, oh, good Mother, as I am thine own, keep me and guard me as thy property and possession" (Prayer of consecration to Mary).

Catholics feel that Mary occupies a unique and tremendously influential position as a result of her role as Christ's human mother. They are taught that they can safely entrust all their problems to her. She provides the spiritual key to salvation of the soul and to receiving miraculous answers to prayers concerning more earthly problems.

Catholics *are* taught (although they will deny this) that Mary is to be given worship equal to God — and higher than that afforded the angels and saints. She is to be addressed as "My Mother." Even casual observation of Catholics reveals that both conversations and services bring forth more references to the "Blessed Virgin" than to the three persons of the Holy Trinity. Obviously, the

Catholic religion *strongly* is oriented toward veneration of Mary. She is called the following:

• The Mother of Divine Grace

• Help of Christians

• Ark of the Covenant

• Queen of Angels

• Morning Star

• Health of the Sick

• The Gate of Heaven

The Catholic "cult of Mary" is based fundamentally on her sacred motherhood. The fourth century title bestowed on her by the church — *Theotokos* (Greek for "Bearer of God") — was equivalent to "Mother of God."

Rome reasoned this way:

"Mary is the mother of Jesus. Jesus is God. Ergo, Mary is the mother of God."

Furthermore, Catholics state and believe that to deny honor to Mary actually is to deny the deity of Christ. Of course, if a person accepts this, he opens a floodgate of ensuing theological absurdities that must be accepted as logical developments of the original fallacy.

IS MARY THE MOTHER OF GOD?

No, Mary is *not* the mother of God. Mary was the mother of the human being, Jesus. Mary served a biological function that was necessary to bring about a *unique* situation. The *preexistent* Son of God was to take on *human* form. As He walked the earth (in human form) He was very God and very man. His "God" component had always been. While Mary was essential to harbor His developing *human* form (for nine months), she had *nothing whatsoever to do with his Godhood!* Mary was, therefore, the mother of Jesus, the man. She was *not,* by any stretch of the imagination, the mother of God.

God has no mother. If one understands the Incarnation, one understands that God, while never ceasing to be God, became completely *man.*

> *"Wherefore when he cometh into the world,*
> *he saith, Sacrifice and offering thou wouldest*
> *not, but a body hast thou prepared me"*
> (Hebrews 10:5).

It was this body that God prepared for His Son — Jesus Christ — who would become man. Of necessity, He would be born into the world as are all other human beings, but with one tremendous difference:

> *"Therefore the Lord himself shall give you*
> *a sign; Behold, a virgin shall conceive, and bear*
> *a son, and shall call his name Immanuel"*
> (Isaiah 7:14).

This virgin was the little teenaged maiden called Mary. She was to bring the Son of God into the world. But it was not God who would be born; it was *"the man Christ Jesus"* (I Timothy 2:5).

THE ANNUNCIATION OF JESUS

The Bible tells us that the Angel Gabriel was sent from God to a virgin named Mary.

"And the angel came in unto her, and said, Hail, thou that art highly favoured, the Lord is with thee: blessed art thou among women" (Luke 1:28).

Using this passage, the Catholic church has altered the words to read: *"Hail, Mary, full of grace."* The church then *interprets* its *own* words by advancing the argument that since Mary *is* full of grace, she must have been the finest and holiest of all created beings. Further, Catholic doctrine concludes that through the grace bestowed on her, she received from God the degree of purity and holiness necessary to be worthy of serving in the role of "Mother of God."

Now, let us pause to examine for a moment the "Hail, Mary" prayer, which is quoted in its entirety at the beginning of this chapter. Because this prayer is based (albeit, loosely) on Scripture (Luke 1:28), it *seems*, to Catholics, to place God's stamp of approval on the Catholic position in regard to Mary.

The "Hail, Mary" begins:

"Hail, Mary, full of grace, the Lord is with thee. Blessed art thou among women and blessed is the fruit of thy womb, Jesus."

WORD USAGE HAS CHANGED

Now, let us digress for a moment to discuss semantics — the study of language. Language changes constantly. Word *meanings* change constantly. For example, a few years ago a person who was "gay" was "happy." Today a "gay" person is a "homosexual," and the old definition has fallen completely out of usage.

By the same token, the word "blessed" has, through usage, taken on two meanings. "Blessed" — pronounced as one syllable — describes someone who has *received* a blessing. When someone is blessed, he has come suddenly into money, he has been cured of an illness, or what-have-you. On the other hand, when pronounced as *two* syllables *(bless-ed)*, the word implies a person of superior spirituality, someone who is more *saintly* in moral character; for example, "that *bless-ed* man returned my lost wallet and wouldn't even accept a reward."

At the time the Bible was written (and when it was translated by the King James translators), the word "blessed" had only *one* meaning — referring to one who had *received* a blessing.

Similarly, the word "grace" has come to have a meaning that *is not* the biblical definition. "Grace" — within Scripture — means a gift from God that is *undeserved*. "Grace" is a free gift from God with no preconditions or strings attached. But today "grace" has come to be used to imply an inherent human quality of goodness that is closely allied to *bless-ed-ness*.

So the wording of the "Hail, Mary" prayer, taken in the context of today's language usage, *appears* to give scriptural support to Catholic contentions that Mary was eternally without sin. Turning to the *actual* words of Scripture, however, we receive a different picture. The Angel Gabriel's actual words were:

> *"Hail, thou that art highly favoured, the Lord is with thee: blessed art thou among women"* (Luke 1:28).

Mary *was* unquestionably highly favored by God in that He chose her to receive this honor. And it was certainly a blessing to be singled out to hold such a distinctive position in the history of the world. But all the rest of the words within this prayer simply were *composed* by the Catholic church and have no basis in Scripture whatsoever.

Delving further into this matter, we read where Mary's cousin Elisabeth said:

> *"And whence is this to me, that the mother of my Lord should come to me?"* (Luke 1:43).

Here Elisabeth called Jesus "Lord." She was talking about the unborn Holy Child then occupying Mary's womb. He definitely is Lord. He is called *"the Lord Jesus Christ"* many times within the Word of God.

But, once again, it must be emphasized that it was not God who was born of Mary, it was the human child — the Lord Jesus Christ.

The unbiblical worship of Mary has its perverted foundation in the insupportable misnomer, "Mother of God." The *correct* scriptural description of Mary is the simple biblical expression, *"Mary the mother of Jesus"* (Acts 1:14).

THE IMMACULATE CONCEPTION

This erroneous (and confusing) term does not refer to the conception of Jesus Christ (as most non-Catholics and many Catholics believe). It refers to the conception of Mary in *her* mother's womb.

The Catholic Catechism says:

"The Blessed Virgin Mary alone, from the first instant of her conception, through the foreseen merits of Jesus Christ, by a unique privilege granted her by God, was kept free from the stain of original sin . . . . From the first moment of her conception (she) possessed justice and holiness, even the fullness of grace, with the infused virtues and the gifts of the Holy Ghost."

This doctrine, a total fiction with *no* scriptural support, was "infallibly" defined by Pope Pius IX as part of the "revealed deposit of Catholic faith" in 1854. There was great opposition to this pronouncement, at the time, within the Catholic church.

The doctrine of the Immaculate Conception implies that for Mary to be born without original sin, her mother also had to be a sinless virgin. The only other alternative is that God granted her a unique *immunity* to the all-pervasive original sin that is an inescapable element of the human condition.

To be frank, Roman Catholic theologians lamely defend their assertion of the Immaculate Conception by saying that "God *could* have done it" or "it was *fitting* that He should do so — and therefore He did it."

But, of course, if God *had* decided on such a course, it would have meant that He was *replacing* the plan of salvation described in the Bible with a totally new concept. *If this* had *happened, we would have a quadrinity instead of the Trinity*. God's Word then would have stated that the Godhead consists of God the Father, God the Son, God the Holy Spirit, and Mary, the Mother of God. The Bible does *not* so state, so we can then conclude that this aberrant doctrine is *not of God*.

THE ORIGIN OF "MARY, THE MOTHER OF GOD"

The veneration of Mary, the Mother of God, and the use of the term "Mother of God" originated *about* A.D. 381. It was officially decreed by the Council of Ephesus in A.D. 431.

Prayers started to be directed to Mary as well as to the other saints *about* A.D. 600.

The "Immaculate Conception of Mary" was proclaimed by Pius IX, as previously stated, in A.D. 1854.

In 1931 Pope Pius XI reaffirmed the doctrine that Mary is the "Mother of God."

In 1950 Pope Pius XII pronounced the doctrine of the "Assumption of Mary." This states that Mary, at the completion of her earthly life, was bodily taken up into heaven without knowing death. Oddly enough, this mystical belief had been a peripheral precept within the Catholic church since the Middle Ages, but was only given official certification in 1950. There was a *great* deal of resistance to the issuance of this doctrine by Pius XII, but he insisted that it was his infallible right to declare such a "fact."

THE BABYLONIAN CULT

Fundamentally, the worship of Mary originated with the worship of "The Queen of Heaven" — a pagan deity. It seems that the Roman church — in altering its doctrines to conform to those formerly observed by conscripted pagans — saw that it would be politically desirable to supply the populace with a satisfying parallel figure within their newly imposed Christian religion. Thus was Mary elevated to divine status.

The image of mother and child had been a primary object of Babylonian worship for centuries before the birth of Christ. From Babylon this spread to the ends of the earth. The original mother figure in this tableau was Semiramis — the personification of unbridled lust and sexual gratification. And once we start to study the worship practices of heathen nations, we find amazing similarities embraced over wide areas and through long periods of time.

For instance: In Egypt, the mother and child are known as Isis and Horus; in India, Isi and Iswara; in Asia, Cybele and Edoius; in Pagan Rome, Fortuna and Jupiter-puer; in Greece, Ceres with Plutus in arms. In isolated Tibet and in China and Japan, early Roman Catholic missionaries were stunned to find counterparts of the Madonna (the Italian name for the Virgin Mary) and her child being worshiped as devoutly as in Rome itself. Shing Moo (the "Mother of China") is represented with child in arms and with a halo around her head — exactly as if she had been painted by a Roman painter.

These nations all trace their common worship from Babylon — before its dispersion in the days of Nimrod. *Thus, worship of Mary is Babylonian in origin. There is absolutely no suggestion of such worship in Scripture.*

MARY AS THE MEDIATOR
BETWEEN JESUS AND MAN

Mary is looked upon by the Catholic church as an intercessor, a mediator, and a redemptress. Some Catholics say this is not a "defined article of the faith." Others say it is. In any case, in practice it is part and parcel of what is known as the "Ordinary Teaching Authority" of the church.

These titles signify that Mary is a *universal intercessor* — that is, she seeks God's favors for all mankind. They clearly imply that Mary is so intimately associated with our redemption that she may be considered a cosaviour with Christ, although subordinate to Him. Church doctrine further alleges that Mary "mediates grace universally."

What does this mean in plain language? Incredibly, the Catholic position is that no grace flows from God to any person without passing through the good offices of Mary!

Some church leaders state that doctrines concerning Mary were modified and tempered by the Second Vatican Council of 1962-1965. However, this is what Catholic Priest Anthony Wildhelm stated in his book, *Christ Among Us: A Modern Presentation of the Catholic Faith*:

• **On page 90:** *"God the Son became a man through Mary, His human mother, whom we call the Mother of God. We can say that God has relatives, that God has a mother."*

• **On page 91:** *"The 'Hail, Mary' is one of the most ancient prayers of the church . . . 'Hail, Mary, full of grace.'*
"By these privileges, which God gave to Mary, we can see that He always prepares people for their roles in His plan."

• **On page 367:** *"We particularly honor Mary, the Mother of Christ, because of her great role in God's plan of salvation. She was closer to Christ than anyone else."*

• **On page 368:** *"Mary is God's masterpiece. To honor her is to honor God, who made her what she is.*
"Because of Mary's great role, she was conceived without sin, remained sinless throughout life, and was perpetually a virgin.
"We believe in Mary's assumption, that she was taken into heaven, body and soul, at the end of her earthly life."

• **On page 369:** *"We give special place to Mary's intercession and sometimes consider her to be our 'spiritual mother.'"*

• **On page 370:** *"Mary is the model Christian, the preeminent member of the church."*

• **On page 371:** *"Mary is particularly the model of our worship.*

"The devotion of the rosary has been a tremendous influence in helping hundreds of millions to pray."

The Roman cult of Mary erects a barrier between the individual and the Trinity. It confuses the Catholic believer's perception of the work and functions of the individual members of the Godhead. It robs Christ of His unique creatorship.

Rome's theologians insist that Mary's role and function is to lead souls to Christ. However, Jesus said:

> *"That which is born of the Spirit is spirit*
> *. . . so is every one that is born of the Spirit"*
> (John 3:6-8).

He further stated:

> *"No man can come to me, except the Father which hath sent me draw him"* (John 6:43, 44).

So, according to the *Bible*, Mary has *no* role to play in the salvation of a soul.

I go back once again to our quote from a former Catholic priest:

"The Jesus I once knew was a wafer of bread and a cup of wine, and He had a mother called Mary who stood between Him and me . . . ."

Does his statement sound like *he* was "led to Christ by Mary"?

DO CATHOLICS WORSHIP MARY?

In scores of letters we have received, Catholics maintain that they do not worship Mary, that she only aids them in their worship of God.

However, when the Catholic attributes the Immaculate Conception to Mary, they are conferring divinity upon her by this claim. The term "worship," as defined by *Webster's New Collegiate Dictionary*, is *"reverence paid to a divine being and extravagant respect or admiration for, or devotion to, an object of esteem."* In ascribing the Immaculate Conception to Mary, the Catholic church has, in effect, declared her divine and thus renders her worship that *should* be reserved only for deity. By their constant reference to her, worship is afforded.

Yes, Catholics *do* worship Mary. To be tragically concise, most Catholics do not understand the worship of God the Father or of His Son, Jesus Christ. The real focus and conception of their worship is directed to Mary. And, of course, their perception of worshiping God is the worship of God *through* Mary. Everything *must go through Mary* to God — and everything must come *from* God through Mary.

MARY AS THE BIBLE DESCRIBES HER

To be brutally frank, there is little mention of Mary within the Word of God.

MATTHEW

In Matthew, Chapter 2, we read of Mary's witnessing the adoration of the wise men. This chapter also recounts the events leading to the trip to Egypt. Then it gives the account of an experience from the childhood of Jesus and describes Mary's concern.

MARK

Mary is mentioned only briefly in this Gospel: once as simply the mother of the Carpenter Jesus (Mark 6:3) and, again, as a family member (Mark 3:32).

LUKE

Luke, Chapter 1, describes the visit of the Angel Gabriel to Mary. The same chapter tells of Mary's visit to Elisabeth. We can conclude from the statements made by Mary that she had a wide-ranging knowledge of the Old Testament — which is a commentary on her spiritual perceptions.

Luke, Chapter 2, describes Mary as giving birth to the Lord Jesus Christ in the stable. She also pondered here the words of the shepherds.

JOHN

In John, Chapter 2, Mary asked Jesus to perform His first public miracle at Cana. (Obviously, because of the confidence with which she approached the situation, she knew His capabilities.) Oddly enough, in Mark 3, Matthew 12, and Luke 8 it seems she either opposed His ministry or at least harbored some confusion about His mission.

John, Chapter 19, talks about how Mary stood at the foot of the cross and observed with great sorrow the death of her Son — her Saviour and our Saviour — the Lord Jesus Christ.

ACTS

According to Acts 1:14 Mary was numbered among the hundred and twenty who tarried in the upper room waiting for the enduement of power on the Day of Pentecost. She, like other believers, needed that infilling of the Holy Spirit as power for service.

This is all the Bible reveals about Mary. (And, incidentally, in the Gospels, Jesus never did call her "mother." He addressed her as "woman." But going back to the ancient Hebrew, this was not an expression of disrespect.)

So, let us look now, without superimposed opinions or doctrines, at the bare bones of what the Bible *does* say about Mary.

HIGHLY FAVORED

When the Angel Gabriel appeared to her, as described in the first chapter of Luke, he used the word *"Hail."* This simply means "hello," a salutation used to get a person's attention. He also used the phrase *"highly favoured,"* which means "blessed" or "endued with grace." As discussed earlier, these terms do not imply any more than that the person has received an unmerited favor.

Mary *was* highly favored. No doubt hundreds of thousands (or even millions) of pious, young Israelite maidens had aspired to be the one so highly favored. They had known, from ancient prophecies, that the "seed," the "redeemer," would be born to a Hebrew maiden. And, from Isaiah's prophecy, they further knew that she had to be a virgin.

*"Therefore the Lord himself shall give you
a sign; Behold, a virgin shall conceive, and bear*

a son, and shall call his name Immanuel''
(Isaiah 7:14).

Very importantly, the lineage had to come through David. Matthew gave the genealogy in the royal line through Solomon. In Luke, the royal line was given from Nathan, another son, through Heli, the father of Mary. Both lines were necessary in fulfilling prophecy.

God had cursed Jechoniah of the royal line and had sworn that no seed of his should ever sit on the throne of David and reign in Jerusalem (Jeremiah 22:24-30).

God had also sworn to David that *his* line (through Solomon) would forever sit on his throne (II Samuel 7). The only way this could be fulfilled was for Jesus, the son of David (through Nathan and Mary), to become legal heir to the throne of David through His stepfather, Joseph, of the kingly line (Luke 1:32, 33).

Jesus, as the foster son of Joseph and the firstborn of his family, became the legal heir to David's throne through Joseph. However, it must be remembered, the royal line in Matthew was given through Solomon, which culminates in Joseph. The royal line in Luke was given through Nathan, culminating in the father of Mary, Heli.

So, Mary, in the royal lineage through Nathan, David's son, became the mother of the Lord Jesus Christ.

Yes, Mary *was* highly favored.

And certainly it could be said that the Lord was with her and she would be blessed among many.

HANDMAIDEN OF THE LORD

Mary called herself ''. . . *the handmaid of the Lord''* (Luke 1:38).

This shows the beautiful humility characterized by Mary and is a statement that might well be studied by Catholic theologians.

However, there is a tremendous difference between "the handmaid of the Lord" *and* "Mother of God."

By her own words Mary refuted the Catholic doctrine of the Immaculate Conception:

> *"And my spirit hath rejoiced in God my* Saviour" (Luke 1:47).

This statement totally discounts the theory of an Immaculate Conception and the Catholic contention that Mary was ever without sin. If God was her Saviour, then she must have needed salvation, which presupposes some history of normal human sin. *No Scripture even hints that Mary was sinless.*

This false cult of Mary worship is another effort by Satan who knows that one cannot completely accept Christ as long as one retains heretical concepts of Mary. Incidentally, Luke's statement in 1:28 quotes Gabriel's words as being *"Blessed art thou* among *women."* It does not say, *"Blessed art thou* above *women."*

ACCORDING TO THE BIBLE, IS MARY AN INTERCESSOR AND A MEDIATRIX?

> *"Wherefore he is able also to save them to the uttermost that come unto God by him, seeing he ever liveth to make intercession for them"* (Hebrews 7:25).

Jesus Christ is our only intercessor. There is no hint or suggestion in the Word of God that Mary should or would occupy such a role. Whenever Mary is inserted into the role of intercessor (as she is by the Catholic church, to intercede with her Son, Jesus Christ, on behalf of individuals on earth), this, in effect, robs Christ of the rightful position He *earned* through His tremendous sacrifice on Calvary. He paid the full price on that cross with the shedding of His precious blood.

Christ alone is worthy to make intercession for us. Christ alone paid the price. Mary did not suffer and die on the cross. She did not shed her blood. And neither does Christ need an *assistant* to motivate Him to intercede for the saints. He is perfectly capable of performing this duty Himself, as He ever sits at the right hand of God making intercession for us.

> *"It is Christ that died, yea rather, that is risen again, who is even at the right hand of God, who also maketh intercession for us"* (Romans 8:34).

There is no hint in the Bible that Christ will have a "staff" to assist Him or that Mary has any role to perform in such a position. There is no need for additional mediators or motivators.

We blaspheme when we imply that Jesus Christ would not satisfactorily accomplish His eternal job without persuasion from His earthly mother.

We blaspheme when we add to the Word of God:

> *"For there is one God, and one mediator between God and men, the man Christ Jesus; Who gave himself a ransom for all"* (I Timothy 2:5, 6).

This states boldly that there is *one God*. We then are told further, in equally clear terms, that there is *one mediator* between God and man.

Please note that fact well.

There are not two mediators, not three or four, just *one*! And then, if there is any confusion, the *identity* of that *one mediator* is revealed:

> *"For there is one God, and one mediator between God and men, the man Christ Jesus"* (I Timothy 2:5).

Why is He the mediator? Again, Scripture spells it out clearly:

> *"Who gave himself a ransom for all"* (I Timothy 2:6).

Obviously, we blaspheme when we intrude Mary (or anyone else) into a mediatory role that is distinctively that of the Lord Jesus Christ alone. And, once again, there is no hint or suggestion in Scripture that any such role ever has been considered for her by God.

The Roman Catholic position is that God the Father and His Son, Jesus Christ, are, through normal human efforts, unreachable. By extension, they then propose that since Christ's mother is available, that petitions delivered by her will not be ignored. Who would turn away his own mother if she came seeking a minor favor?

Thus, in Catholic tradition, when a person goes through the mother, he gets through more quickly and more surely. No doubt Jesus will look with more favor on *her* requests than on any delivered directly. Hence, those bumper stickers: *"CAN'T FIND JESUS? LOOK FOR HIS MOTHER."*

Such statements totally misinterpret the person of God and the incarnation, redemption, and plan of God for the human race. The Apostle Paul said it well:

> *"Now the Spirit speaketh expressly, that in the latter times some shall depart from the faith, giving heed to seducing spirits, and doctrines of devils; Speaking lies in hypocrisy; having their conscience seared with a hot iron; Forbidding to marry, and commanding to abstain from meats, which God hath created to be received with thanksgiving of them which believe and know the truth"* (I Timothy 4:1).

In all the Early Church no statement is reported of an apostle referring to Mary as the "Mother of God." There is no hint of prayers being offered to her, nor admonitions given to the saints to honor her beyond what the Bible suggests as normal deference.

Surely, if this great fabrication were valid, we would have at least a *word* from the Early Church concerning Mary.

The silence is deafening!

CHAPTER SEVEN

THE WORSHIP OF SAINTS AND IMAGES

he worship of saints and images is an integral part of the Roman Catholic religion. Let us examine it as the Roman Catholic church teaches and proclaims it — and then let us look at it in the light of the Word of God.

THE TEACHING OF THE ROMAN CATHOLIC CHURCH TODAY

The Roman Catholic church teaches that . ˙. .

- The saints function as mediators between the faithful and God.

- We should address prayers to the saints and kneel before them to obtain their favor.

- The saints are pleased to see their images venerated and adorned with costly treasures, and they will recompense the faithful who are generous in their worship.

- The images of the Blessed Virgin and the Lord Jesus Christ may be venerated under different names. This can give rise to competition between different *images* of the *same person*.

- According to the Catholic position, "saints" are individuals of the New Testament (or later martyrs or notable persons of "The Church") who have died and subsequently been declared to be saints by the pope.

A GREAT PROBLEM

In this enlightened age it is difficult to realize that the majority of Catholics are unaware of the direct contradiction between a belief in an omnipotent God and the worship of saints as advocates and intercessors.

In a conversation between an Evangelical and several Roman Catholics, the following inquiry was raised:

"Everyone accepts that the saints are finite beings — not only on earth but in heaven as well. So how can finite beings hear the prayers of men who are on the earth? If one would stop to think about this, it would seem impossible for a finite being to hear the prayers of not just two or three people, but those of multiplied thousands who are all praying at the same time.

"The only way they could hear so many thousands of prayers, and discern the heart attitudes of all of these people, is if they were both omniscient and omnipresent. In other words, each saint would have to be God in order to accomplish this."

When this question was put to the Roman Catholic representatives, they did not know how to reply. Finally, after a whispered conference, one of them offered:

"There is no difficulty. Even if the saints can't hear our prayers, God can and He could reveal them to the saints."

Dare we anticipate the resulting conclusion in this dialogue?

This would then mean that we would be approaching the saints through God — instead of God through the saints.

The idea becomes more absurd the further we pursue it.

The very thought of individuals speaking to frail and finite humans — and expecting them to carry their ideas to God — is ludicrous. The Word of God states clearly that we can go directly to the Father, at any time, in the name of the Lord Jesus Christ (John 16:23).

WHERE DID THE CATHOLIC WORSHIP OF SAINTS AND IMAGES ORIGINATE?

The Catholic system of patron saints is nothing more nor less than a continuation of ancient heathen beliefs in gods devoted to days, occupations, and the various needs of human life. Since the worship of saints is really a perpetuation of these false gods, Romanism is patently guilty of worshiping *other gods* — a practice that is condemned repeatedly in Scripture.

By the tenth century some twenty-five thousand saints had been canonized by the Roman Catholic church. Of course, by this time Rome had hopelessly insinuated pagan religions into Christianity.

SUBSTITUTE A CHRISTIAN-SOUNDING NAME

To make the apostasy less obvious, the leaders of the Roman Catholic church substituted Christian-sounding names that were similar to the original pagan names.

For example, the goddess Victoria of the Basses-Alps was renamed St. Victoire. The pagan god Osiris was renamed St. Onuphris. Apollo was renamed St. Apollinaris, and the heathen god Mars became St. Martine.

We are told that one of the best preserved of the ancient temples in Rome is the Pantheon, which was originally dedicated to "Jove and all the gods." It was *re*consecrated, however, by Pope Boniface IV to the "Mother of God and all the saints." An edifice formerly consecrated to the Greek god Apollo now is displayed proudly as the Church of St. Apollinaris.

Where the ancient temple of Mars once stood, we now find the Church of St. Martine. Rome simply *adopted* the heathen gods into the so-called Christian church, renaming them as their worship continued uninterrupted.

Just as the pagans worshiped idols or statues of their gods, so does the Roman Catholic church utilize statues in their worship.

In many cases the *same statue* that was worshiped as a pagan god was rechristened with the name of a Christian saint, and worship continued. The statue of Jupiter, for example, was slightly changed and retitled "Peter."

Through the centuries more and more statues have been crafted (and venerated) until today there are churches in Europe that contain as many as several *thousand* statues! However, whether in a great cathedral, a small chapel, or on the dashboard of an automobile, these are still idols and are absolutely forbidden by the Word of God.

NOT THE HINT OF SUCH IN
SCRIPTURE OR IN THE EARLY CHURCH

It was not until the fifth century that pictures of Mary, Christ, and the saints were made and used as objects of worship.

Scripture specifically condemns idol worship in countless places, as there is not a hint or a suggestion in the Word of God that the Early Church deviated from these age-old injunctions.

THE VOICE OF THE ELDERS
IN THE EARLY CHURCH

Irenaeus (*about* A.D. 130-202), a pupil of Polycarp (who sat at the feet of the Apostle John), said:

"As the church has received liberally from the Lord, so let it minister liberally, and not ask to do anything through the invocation of angels or through enchantments and other perverse rarities, but let prayers be addressed purely, clearly, and openly to the Lord, from whom are all things, invoking the name of our Lord Jesus Christ."

Clement of Alexandria, a Greek theologian (*about* A.D. 150-215), said:

"It is the height of foolishness to pray as though to gods to those who are no gods at all, for there is but one good God, to Him only do we and the angels pray."

In another place he said:

"Every image or statue should be called an idol for it is nothing but vile and profane material, and for this reason and to remove idolatry by the roots, God has forbidden the use of any image or likeness of anything in heaven or on earth, and has also forbidden the making of such images, and for this reason we Christians have none of these material representations."

Origen, Greek teacher and writer (*about* A.D. 185-254), said:

"The angels are greatly interested in your salvation. They have been given as helpers to the Son of God, but all prayers to God, whether they are supplications or thanksgiving, should be raised to Him through Christ, the High Priest, who is above all angels . . . men do not know the angels so it is unreasonable to address prayers to them instead of to Christ who is known of men. And even were we to know the angels, we should not be allowed to address our prayers to anyone except to God, the Lord of all creation, who is sufficient for all, and we come to Him through our Saviour, the Son of God."

The same writer said in another place:

"In the reproof of those who trust in the saints, I would say, 'cursed be the man that trusteth in man' *(Jeremiah 17:5), and* 'It is better to trust in the Lord than to put confidence in man' *(Psalm 118:8). If it is necessary for us to have confidence in anyone, let us leave all others and trust in the Lord."*

Cyprian (martyred *about* A.D. 258), bishop of Carthage (*about* 248-258), declared:

"Why bow down before images? Lift up your eyes and heart to heaven; that is the place where you should seek God."

Athanasius, a bishop at Alexandria and the father of orthodoxy (*about* A.D. 300-373), said:

"It is written, 'God [*is*] my rock; in him will I trust; he is my shield, and the horn of my salvation' *(II Samuel 22:3), and* 'The Lord also will be a refuge for the oppressed, a refuge in times of trouble' *(Psalm 9:9). And how many similar words do we find in the Sacred Scriptures! Should anyone reply that these are prophecies that apply to the Son, which may be true, then let them admit that the saints do not venture to call any created being their help and refuge."*

Elsewhere he declared:

"The invocation of idols is a sin, and anything that is sinful at the beginning can never be good later."

Augustine, bishop of Hippo (*about* A.D. 354-430), said:

"Let not our religion be the worship of the dead, for if they lived a holy life, it is impossible to imagine that they desire such honours, rather they would wish that we should render our worship to Him through whom we should be partakers with them of salvation. Therefore we should honor them by imitating them — not by worshiping them.

"The only image of Christ that we should make for ourselves is to keep before us His humility, patience, and kindness, and endeavor to make our lives like His in all things. Those who go in search of Jesus and the apostles in mural paintings, far from conforming to Scripture, fall into error."

Jerome (*about* 343-420), who translated the Old Testament directly into Latin from Hebrew (the Vulgate Bible), quoted a letter from Epiphanius in which he stated the following:

"In a part of the country that I visited I found a candle placed in the door of a church over which was painted an image of Christ and another of a saint. I was displeased that, in this defiance of Holy Scripture, the image of a man should be hung up in the church of Christ, and I cut the candle down, advising the sacristan that it would be put to better use at the funeral of some poor person."

THE USE OF IMAGES
CONDEMNED BY MANY

The use of images was condemned by all in the Early Church and even condemned as late as the Synod of Elvira

(A.D. 305), the Council of Frankfort (A.D. 794), and the
Council of Rouen (A.D. 1445). This latter assembly in its
seventh canon condemned the practice of praying before
images with names such as Our Lady of Piety, Our Lady of
Help, or Our Lady of Consolation.

It said:

*"Such practices tend to lead to superstition, as though
there were more power in some than in others."*

Desiderius Erasmus of Rotterdam (*about* 1466-1536),
a Dutch scholar held in high esteem by the Roman Catholic
church, was right when he said:

*"No one who bows before an image or looks at it
intentionally is free from some kind of superstition; and
not only so, but if he only prays before an image."*

THE FOLLOWING ILLUSTRATIONS OF SUPERSTITION AND PRAYING TO SAINTS WERE COPIED FROM A ROMAN CATHOLIC PAPER PUBLISHED IN 1930

• *Two gossips were talking in confidential tones to
each other at the end of the street. "What troubles we've been
through! You know all about it. But listen, I put great
confidence in Our Lady of Purity and I've committed all
our troubles to her."*

*"You don't mean to say," said the other, "that you've
gone to Our Lady of Purity? Why, I would never confide in
her, that would be the last thing I would do."*

"Why ever not?" asked her companion.

*"Well, look. I always confide in The Mother of the God
of Sorrows. She has been through great affliction and
understands my troubles. I wouldn't have the same confidence in Our Lady of Purity — she lacks experience!"*

• *A young woman entered a church as an older woman
with bowed shoulders and wrinkled skin was coming out.*

"Good morning, Grandmother. How early you are today."

"Yes, you are right. Seven months ago I promised the Virgin of Sorrows to take her a taper and I have at last taken it. But what a problem! I had to pass in front of the Virgin of the Rosary, and I was so afraid that she might notice that I was taking the taper to the other one. I hid it under my apron as I passed by, but even so I am afraid she may have seen it. What a trial! And we are too poor to afford one for each."

WHAT DOES THE BIBLE SAY?

"Ye shall make you no idols nor graven image, neither rear you up a standing image, neither shall ye set up any image of stone in your land, to bow down unto it: for I am the Lord your God" (Leviticus 26:1).

"Be not deceived: neither fornicators, nor idolaters . . . shall inherit the kingdom of God" (I Corinthians 6:9, 10).

"For there is one God, and one mediator between God and men, the man Christ Jesus" (I Timothy 2:5).

"Neither is there salvation in any other: for there is none other name under heaven given among men, whereby we must be saved" (Acts 4:12).

With regard to the worship of the saints we read:

"And as Peter was coming in, Cornelius met him, and fell down at his feet, and worshipped him. But Peter took him up, saying, Stand up; I myself also am a man" (Acts 10:25, 26).

*"And I John saw these things, and heard them. And when I had heard and seen, I fell down to worship before the feet of the angel which shewed me these things. Then saith he unto me, See thou do it not: for I am thy fellow-servant, and of thy brethren the prophets, and of them which keep the sayings of this book: worship **God**"* (Revelation 22:8, 9).

ALL TRUE CHRISTIANS ARE SAINTS

There is no indication in the Word of God that a person becomes a saint *after* he dies. In fact, it is not the pope who makes someone a saint, it is God. In Scripture, saints are always living people — never the dead.

For example, when Paul wrote to the Ephesians, his letter was addressed *"to the saints which are at Ephesus"* (Ephesians 1:1).

Likewise, the book of Philippians was written *"to all the saints in Christ Jesus which are at Philippi"* (Philippians 1:1).

The early Christians in the church at Rome were called *"saints"* (Romans 1:7; 16:15), as were the Christians who lived at Corinth (I Corinthians 1:2; II Corinthians 1:1).

Consequently, if a person wants a saint to pray for him, he should find a Christian and ask him to join him in prayer, for *all true Christians are saints*.

Anytime a person tries to contact people who have died, it is a form of spiritualism. The Bible repeatedly condemns any attempt to commune with the dead.

> *"There shall not be found among you . . .*
> *an enchanter [one who uses incantations], or a*
> *witch, Or a charmer, or a consulter with familiar*
> *spirits, or a wizard, or a necromancer [one who*
> entreats the spirits of the dead]. *For all that do*
> *these things are an abomination unto the Lord"*
> (Deuteronomy 18:10-12).

> *"When they shall say unto you, Seek unto*
> *them that have familiar spirits, and unto wizards*
> *that peep, and that mutter: should not a people*
> *seek unto their God? for the living to the dead?*
> *. . . if they speak not according to this word, it is*
> *because there is no light in them"* (Isaiah 8:19, 20).

WHAT ABOUT THE MIRACLES
AND THE SHRINES?

I am sure, after reading this, that some will say, "But what about the miracles that have been performed by the intercession of the saints?"

These consist of statues that weep, form tears on faces, or produce (alleged) miracles. The Virgin of Lourdes is the most publicized.

Actually, there is absolutely *nothing* in the Word of God that even *hints* at such a thing. God has never healed or performed miracles or done any kind of good works through inanimate objects, except in the case of Paul's handkerchiefs and aprons, as described in Acts 19:12. And this one isolated case is *not* an example of worshiping or venerating an idol or image.

If a person were to visit Lourdes today, he would be appalled by the carnival atmosphere. This is, of course, totally foreign to the Word of God and the *work* of God. There are no miracles at Lourdes, no healings or cures or anything else of this nature. There may be emotional reactions, but that is as far as it goes.

However, this should be said as well.

Satan, who causes sicknesses by demon oppression (Acts 10:38; Luke 13:11-16) can take off what he puts on without opposing himself or casting himself out. When he can damn a soul by getting a person to deny the essentials of the Bible that will save the soul, then it is to his advantage to deceive by taking away the sickness.

SATAN DECEIVES PEOPLE

Many accept false religions that promise healing and other benefits. Satan cooperates with these religions which he himself has founded to deceive men. He can even bring about a withdrawal of the sickness from people without God being involved in the process. Such people naturally think they are in the true religion. They reject Christ and see no need of being saved from sin or of following Christianity. They will be damned for doing so, Satan having won their souls.

One of the major works of Satan is the work of deception, and, in this vein, along with other efforts, he is leading much of the world astray.

Yes, we do believe in miracles. We believe in healing. We believe that God answers prayer. But we believe that it comes about in a biblical way.

Jesus said a long time ago:

> *"Come unto me [*Jesus Himself — not some angel or dead saint*] . . . and I will give you rest.*

Take my yoke upon you, and learn of me [not
some angel or dead saint] . . . *and ye shall find*
rest unto your souls'' (Matthew 11:28, 29).

IN CLOSING

God uses living men and women to pray for the sick —
and He does answer prayer when it is offered according to
His Holy Word.

> *''Is any sick among you? let him call for the*
> *elders of the church; and let them pray over him,*
> *anointing him with oil in the name of the Lord:*
> *And the prayer of faith shall save the sick, and*
> *the Lord shall raise him up''* (James 5:14).

The worship of saints and images has absolutely no
foundation in the Word of God. It is an excursion into
superstition and paganism, which will further enfold its
web of deceit around the follower of Roman Catholicism.

> *''In that day ye shall ask me nothing.*
> *Verily, verily, I say unto you, Whatsoever ye*
> *shall ask the Father in my name, he will give it*
> *you. Hitherto have ye asked nothing in my*
> *name: ask, and ye shall receive, that your joy*
> *may be full. . . . For the Father himself loveth you,*
> *because ye have loved me, and have believed that I*
> *came out from God''* (John 16:23, 24, 27).

CHAPTER EIGHT

THE CANON OF THE BIBLE

 t the end of the first Christian century, the Jewish rabbis, at the Council of Gamnia, closed the canon of Hebrew books (those books considered authoritative). Their decision resulted from . . .

- The multiplication and popularity of sectarian apocryphal writings.

- The fall of Jerusalem (A.D. 70) which created a threat to the religious tradition of the Jews.

- The disputes with Christians over their interpretation of the Jewish Scriptures in preaching and writing.

There was never any doubt about the five books of the Law (Pentateuch), but beyond that, various sects of Judaism disagreed. The prophetic collection was generally agreed upon by 200 B.C., but the major problem concerned the *other writings.* Four criteria operated in deciding what books should occupy a place in the authoritative Old Testament Scriptures:

- The content of each book had to harmonize with the Law.

- Since prophetic inspiration was believed to have begun with Moses (*about* 1450 B.C.) and ended with Ezra (*about* 450 B.C.), to qualify for the canon and to be considered inspired, a book had to have been written within that time frame.

- The language of the original manuscript had to be Hebrew.

- The book had to have been written within the geographical boundaries of Palestine.

On this basis the thirty-nine books of the Old Testament were selected for the Palestinian canon of Scriptures. Failing these criteria, the rest of the ancient Jewish writings came to be classified as *Apocrypha*, or *pseudepigrapha* (literally, "false writings").

A number of Christian writings, other than those that came to be accepted for the New Testament, appeared early and were considered by some to be worthy of canonical status. The Didache, the Epistle of Barnabas, I and II Clement, the Shepherd of Hermes, the Apocalypse of Peter, and the Acts of Paul were some of the more popular ones. By the beginning of the third century, twenty-two of the writings of our present New Testament had been widely accepted.

Four principles, or considerations, were operative in determining what books should occupy a place in the authoritative New Testament Scriptures:

- Was the book written by an apostle — or by someone associated with an apostle?
- Was the book's content of a spiritual nature?
- Was the book widely received by the churches?
- Was there evidence in the book of divine inspiration?

As far as is known, it was the Easter letter of Archbishop Athanasius of Alexandria in A.D. 367 that first listed the twenty-seven books of our New Testament as authoritative. Jerome, by his Latin translation of these same twenty-seven books (A.D. 382), further established this list as canonical for the churches.

This is a brief explanation of how our Bible (thirty-nine books in the Old Testament and twenty-seven in the New Testament) came to be established as the Word of God.

THE APOCRYPHA

This group of books, numbering about fourteen, is believed to be spurious; literally, "false writings." This in no way implies that the books do not contain some good things, nor does it mean they were written by evil men. It simply means they were *not* believed to be inspired; consequently, they were not placed in the canon of Scripture.

Eleven of these Apocryphal books have been accepted by the Catholic church, included in Roman Catholic canon, and placed in the Douay version of the Bible (Catholic).

WHY WERE THESE BOOKS NOT CONSIDERED INSPIRED OR CANONICAL (INCLUDED IN THE CANON, OR BOOKS, OF THE BIBLE)?

Some of the reasons will relate to the Old Testament, some to the New Testament.

- As far as the Old Testament was concerned, these particular books were not included in the Hebrew canon of Scripture.

- The Master, the Apostle Paul, nor any other writer in the New Testament ever quoted from these spurious writings (or Apocrypha). Yet they quoted frequently in the New Testament from the books that were included in the Hebrew canon of Scripture.

- Josephus, the Hebrew historian, expressly *excluded* these "false writings" or Apocrypha.

- None of the Apocryphal books claim divine inspiration.

- The Apocryphal books have historical, geographical, and chronological errors.

- For the most part, they teach and uphold doctrines that are contrary to the Scriptures (for instance, *lying* is sanctioned in some cases, magic is advocated and practiced in other cases, etc.).

- As literature, they are considered to be myth and legend.

- Their spiritual (and even moral) stance generally is far below both the Old and New Testaments.

- Respecting the Old Testament, most of these spurious books were written much later than the books that were considered to be authoritative and inspired.

- As we discussed (in the explanation earlier respecting the New Testament writings), to be canonized a book had to have been written by an apostle or someone associated with an apostle. The book had to be spiritual, had to have been widely received by the churches, and had to show evidence of divine inspiration.

Satan has done everything within his power to hinder, destroy, dilute, and outright do away with the Word of Almighty God. But through the power of God, the Bible as we have it today — its sixty-six books, both Old and New Testaments, from Genesis to Revelation — is the Word of God. Nothing else can be added to it. When any person or any church claims that other writings, other books, other (so-called) inspirations should be included in the canon of Scripture, this is a work of the evil one himself.

The Apostle Paul put it aptly, I think, when he said:

"But though we, or an angel from heaven, preach any other gospel unto you than that which we have preached unto you, let him be accursed. As we said before, so say I now again, If any man preach any other gospel unto you than that ye have received, let him be accursed" (Galatians 1:8, 9).

INFANT BAPTISM: A SCRIPTURAL DOCTRINE?

nfant baptism is not a scriptural doctrine, and more probably, infant baptism is responsible for sending more people to hell than perhaps any other doctrine or religious error.

It is a terrible thing when a person has been led to believe that his being baptized as a baby constitutes his salvation, and consequently he is on his way to heaven.

JESUS AND THE CHILDREN

The fact of how much Jesus loves children was evidenced when He made this statement:

"Suffer little children, and forbid them not, to come unto me: for of such is the kingdom of heaven" (Matthew 19:14).

As we have said so many times, we believe all babies and children below the age of accountability are protected by the Lord respecting their eternal soul. I do not believe that any child below the age of accountability has ever gone to hell. Of course, there is no differentiating between those who were baptized as infants and those who were not.

HISTORY OF INFANT BAPTISM

Infant baptism appeared in church history around the year A.D. 370. It came about as a result of the doctrine of baptismal regeneration — the teaching that baptism is essential to salvation; or, if you want to turn it around, that water baptism saves the soul (or at least is a part of a person's salvation). Consequently, as the teaching of baptismal regeneration started being propagated, it was natural for those holding to this doctrine to believe that everyone should be baptized as soon as possible. Thus, baptism of infants still in the innocent state (and as yet unaccountable for their actions) came into vogue among many of the churches.

Once again I state: *These two grievous errors — baptismal regeneration and infant baptism — have probably caused more people to go to hell than any other doctrine.*

MORE HISTORY

The professed conversion of Emperor Constantine in A.D. 313 was looked upon by many as a great triumph for Christianity. However, it more than likely was the greatest tragedy in church history because it resulted in the union of church and state and the establishment of a hierarchy which ultimately developed into the Roman Catholic system. There is great question that Constantine was ever truly converted. At the time of his *supposed* vision of the sign of the cross, he *promised* to become a Christian. But he was not baptized in water until near death, having postponed the act in the belief that baptism washed away all past sins, and he wanted all of his sins to be in the past tense before he was baptized.

In other words, Constantine wanted the freedom to sin as much as he wanted, and, then, when he was too old or too sick to care, he would have them all washed away by the act of baptism.

In A.D. 416 infant baptism was made compulsory throughout the Roman Empire. Naturally this filled the churches with unconverted members who had only been "baptized into favor." So whatever power the church had in the past relative to actual conversions was now null and void. The world consequently was plunged into the gloom of the Dark Ages which endured for more than twelve centuries — until the Protestant Reformation.

During this time God had a remnant who remained faithful to Him; they never consented to the union of church and state, or to baptismal regeneration, or to infant baptism. These people were called by various names, but probably could better be summed up by their generic name, *Anabaptists,* meaning rebaptizers. These people ignored infant baptism and rebaptized those who had been saved through personal faith. They also had a generic name for themselves — *Antipedobaptists,* meaning "against infant baptism."

NOW THIS IS STRANGE

The strange thing about these two diabolical doctrines of baptismal regeneration and infant baptism is that the great reformers (Martin Luther, for one) brought with them out of Rome these two dreaded errors — the union of church and state and infant baptism. Strangely enough, in those days not only did the Roman Catholic church persecute those who would not conform to its ways, but after the Lutheran church became the established church of Germany, it persecuted the nonconformists as well — of course, not as stringently so and not in such numbers as those before them.

John Calvin in France, as well as Oliver Cromwell in England and John Knox in Scotland, stuck to the union of church and state and infant baptism and used their power, when they had power, to seek to force others to conform to their own views.

Unaware to a lot of people, this thing came to the Americas well in the early days of this republic. Before the Massachusetts Bay Colony was twenty years old, the following was decreed by statute:

"If any person or persons within this jurisdiction shall either openly condemn or oppose the baptizing of infants, or go about secretly to seduce others from the approbation or use thereof, or shall purposely depart from the congregation at the administration of the ordinance — after due time and means of conviction — every such person or persons shall be subject to banishment."

Religious persecution existed even in the early days of the United States of America. Roger Williams and others were banished — when banishment meant to go and live with the Indians — because they would not submit to the doctrine of baptismal regeneration or the baptizing of infants.

However, it was the constitution of the Rhode Island Colony — founded by Roger Williams, John Clark, and others — that established religious liberty by law for the first time in thirteen hundred years (over the world). Thus it was that Rhode Island, founded by a small group of believers, was the first spot on earth where religious liberty became the law of the land. The settlement was made in

1638, and the colony was legally established in 1663. Virginia followed, to be the second, in 1786.

As you can see, the doctrine of infant baptism has a long and bloody history, and it has been one of Satan's chief weapons to condemn untold millions to hell.

I WILL ATTEMPT TO EXPLAIN IT FURTHER

Many, of course, will ask, "What does the above have to do with us today?"

A lot!

You see, the union of church and state continues today in most countries of the world. In these state churches, pastors and leaders christen babies — which means they "make them Christians" by baptizing them; thus the one that has been christened as a baby believes he is on his way to heaven simply because he was christened (or baptized) in infancy. Having been taught all his life that this saved him, he naturally considers himself saved by the act of infant baptism.

The Roman Catholic church teaches baptismal regeneration and practices infant baptism. Its statement of doctrine says:

"The sacrament of baptism is administered on adults by the pouring of water and the pronouncement of the proper words, and cleanses from original sin."

The Reformed church says:

"Children are baptized as heirs of the Kingdom of God and of His covenant."

The Lutheran church teaches that baptism, whether of infants or adults, is a means of regeneration.

Because of the following declaration, I believe the Episcopal church teaches that salvation comes through infant baptism. In his confirmation, the catechist answers a question about his baptism in infancy by saying this:

"In my baptism . . . I was made a member of Christ, a child of God, and an inheritor of the kingdom of God."

(This is printed in the prayer book and can be read by anyone interested enough to look for it.)

Most people who practice infant baptism believe the ceremony has something to do with the salvation of the child. These are traditions of men, and we can follow the commandments of God or follow after the traditions of men; it is up to us.

THE CLEAR BIBLE TEACHING OF SALVATION

I believe the Word of God is clear regarding the matter of salvation. Jesus said:

> *"He that believeth on him is not condemned: but he that believeth not is condemned already, because he hath not believed in the name of the only begotten Son of God . . . He that believeth on the Son hath everlasting life: and he that believeth not the Son shall not see life; but the wrath of God abideth on him"* (John 3:18, 36).

Basically this tells us that there are two groups of people in the world today — those who believe on the Son and those who do not. Those who believe are not condemned; they have everlasting life (whatever church they may belong to). Those who believe not on the Son are condemned already, and they shall not see life, but the wrath of God abides on them.

I believe this is the clear, unmistakable teaching and language of the Bible.

If you will notice, the Word of God never says simply believe and be saved; rather, it seeks always to identify the object of faith, which is the Lord Jesus Christ Himself.

*"For God so loved the world, that he gave
his only begotten Son, that whosoever believeth
in him should not perish, but have everlasting
life"* (John 3:16).

It is not enough just to believe; a person must believe
"in him."

The Philippian jailer asked, *"Sirs, what must I do to be
saved?"* The Apostle Paul answered, *"Believe on the Lord
Jesus Christ, and thou shalt be saved"* (Acts 16:30, 31).

It was not enough simply to believe; that belief, that
trust, that dependence had to be *"in him."*

If a person is trusting in baptism for salvation, he
cannot be trusting *"in him."* Christ is not *one* way of
salvation; He is the *only* way of salvation.

*"Verily, verily, I say unto you, He that
entereth not by the door into the sheepfold, but
climbeth up some other way, the same is a thief
and a robber . . . . Verily, verily, I say unto
you, I am the door of the sheep . . . . I am the
door: by me if any enter in, he shall be saved,
and shall go in and out, and find pasture . . . .
I am the way, the truth, and the life: no
man cometh unto the Father, but by me"*
(John 10:1, 7, 9; 14:6).

There is no promise in the Word of God to those who
believe *partially* in Christ. In other words, we cannot trust
the Lord Jesus Christ 90 percent and baptism 10 percent,
or Jesus 50 percent and baptism 50 percent, or Jesus
95 percent and some church 5 percent, etc. As a matter of
fact, there is no such thing as partially trusting Christ. The
man who is partially trusting is not trusting at all. Yet the
sad fact is that the majority of people in churches in the

United States and the world today are not trusting Christ at all — they *believe* they are trusting Him partially.

It is even sadder to realize that more people are going to hell through religious organizations than any other way. That is a shocking, startling statement, but it is true. Jesus said:

> *"Many will say to me in that day, Lord, Lord, have we not prophesied in thy name? and in thy name have cast out devils? and in thy name done many wonderful works? And then will I profess unto them, I never knew you: depart from me, ye that work iniquity"* (Matthew 7:22, 23).

You see, any works offered to Christ for salvation are called by Jesus Himself, ''works of iniquity.''

There is an old song that expresses my feelings totally:

> *''My hope is built on nothing less*
> *Than Jesus' blood and righteousness;*
> *I dare not trust the sweetest frame,*
> *But wholly lean on Jesus' name.*
> *On Christ, the solid Rock, I stand;*
> *All other ground is sinking sand,*
> *All other ground is sinking sand.''*

Note: *Portions of source material for this chapter were derived from a message by the late Dr. William Pettingill, entitled ''Infant Baptism.''*

CHRISTMAS OR CHRIST-MASS?

 ach year millions of people celebrate the Christmas holiday — and the birth of Christ. But I would ask the question: What is *actually* being celebrated?

Sad to say, Christmas has become so commercialized that few people, even Christians, scarcely realize the true import of most of the traditions surrounding this hallowed time.

As we look deeper into this subject, some disturbing facts will be brought forth — facts that have been suppressed for centuries, yet facts that every true Christian should understand to evaluate properly his own attitude respecting this special season, Christmas. Facts revealed within this chapter will disturb many people, but truth remains truth, and as God's Word says:

> *"If ye continue in my word, then are ye my disciples indeed; And ye shall know the truth, and the truth shall make you free"* (John 8:31, 32).

CHRISTMAS LOOKED AT IN THREE DIFFERENT WAYS

Christmas is, by and large, looked at in one of three ways: the biblical context, the framework of commercialism, or the perspective of its heathen origins. First, let us look at it within the biblical context.

> *"And it came to pass in those days, that there went out a decree from Caesar Augustus, that all the world should be taxed. (And this taxing was first made when Cyrenius was governor of Syria.) And all went to be taxed, every one into his own city. And Joseph also went up from Galilee, out of the city of Nazareth, into Judaea, unto the city of David, which is called Bethlehem; (because he was of the house and lineage of David:) To be taxed with Mary his espoused wife, being great with child. And so it was, that, while they were there, the days were accomplished that she should be delivered. And she brought forth her firstborn son, and wrapped him in swaddling clothes, and laid him in a manger; because there was no room for them in the inn"* (Luke 2:1-7).

This beautiful narrative, given by Luke and confirmed by Matthew, causes the breasts of all true Christians to swell with joy. This is the account of the incarnation of God, His coming to dwell with men. We should celebrate this and we should rejoice in it, for it is only because of this momentous event that man can come forward to be saved.

Even though it is highly improbable that Jesus Christ was born on December 25 (no one can pinpoint precisely the date on which He was born), there is nothing wrong in observing this blessed event on December 25. However, every Christian should realize that this particular date was not chosen as a matter of sheer coincidence. There were definite reasons for choosing this date as a major religious holiday, and we will discuss this more fully in a moment.

Before getting into the true roots of many of our religious observances, I want to emphasize that the average Christian celebrates the birth of our Lord in worship and in praise, in glorifying God and thanking Him for sending His Son to serve as the atonement for every man's sin. Without Him, and without this unique moment when God became man, we would all die lost. Therefore, not only is the celebration of Christ's birth scriptural, but it is altogether fitting and proper that we should, at some time during the year, pay special homage to this event and celebrate it with joy, with thanksgiving, and — particularly — with reverence.

When we worship the Lord and celebrate Christmas in this spirit, we are doing so biblically and correctly. Yet the sad fact is, for most people Christmas is just one more in a succession of worldly highs and is obscenely commercialized. All too many people observe this season for one reason only: the ringing of the cash register. Of course, there is nothing inherently wrong with showing a profit, and there is nothing wrong with merchants prospering as the public observes Christmas; but, at the same time, when we lose the true meaning of Christmas, we lose all that really matters.

It would be good if all Christians would set aside a time for quiet retrospection as to their own personal motives in regard to the holidays. Each should define within his own heart whether Christmas is notable because it is the biggest business time of the year (which it is) or because it memorializes the single most important event in the history of the world (which it most assuredly does).

Beyond this basic question, however, there is even more to be explored in relationship to the Christmas season. Sad to say, there is a pagan side to the celebration of Christmas, and this is basically what this chapter is all about. I think we should look seriously at this, without prejudice or preconceived ideas, and delve into the true background of this winter holiday — for I believe that true worship can be based only upon truth. Therefore, I ask you to consider *prayerfully* all that will follow. Although disturbing, these observations are (we believe), nonetheless, truths.

A HEATHEN FESTIVAL

Actually, Christmas (or more literally, "Christmass") was the direct adoption of a heathen festival observed on December 24 and 25 in honor of the son of the Babylonian queen, Astarte. Observed for centuries before Christ (a fact that is well documented), the Chaldeans called this "yule day" or "child day."

The Christmas tree that we accept without question was well known in pre-Christian, pagan times and was common to all tribes. According to one legend, on the eve of the day (December 24), the Yule log was cast into a tree, from which divine gifts appeared — presents from the gods to bless men in the new year. This tree was common in the days of Jeremiah, who expressly warned Israel to forsake this heathen custom.

"Learn not the way of the heathen. . . . For the customs of the people are vain: for one cutteth a tree out of the forest, the work of the hands of the workman, with the axe. They deck it with silver and with gold; they fasten it with nails and with hammers, that it move not. They are upright as the palm tree, but speak not. . . . they are all the work of cunning men. But the Lord is the true God, he is the living God, and an everlasting king" (Jeremiah 10:1-9).

There is no indication whatsoever that Christ was born on December 25. Rather, from everything found in Scripture, we must conclude that He was born during the warmer months of the year. For one thing, we know He was laid in a manger (outside, or at least in an unheated stable). The cold months in Israel (from December to February) are generally too severe for traveling to pay a tax, as Joseph did with his family. All travel in those days was by foot or, leastways, by primitive means.

Scripture also tells us that shepherds were in the fields. Although there are times when shepherds *could have been* in the fields at this time of year, it is *unlikely* that they were out in the open with their flocks during the winter months.

We know further that the apostles did not observe the day we do as Christ's birthday. Tertullian, writing in the middle of the third century, lamented the fact that Christians were beginning to observe the customs of the heathen in this regard. He said:

"Gifts are carried to and fro, New Year's Day presents are made with din, and sports and banquets are celebrated with uproar."

The church structure, full of pagans since the reign of Constantine, became so corrupt in its effort to recruit ever more to church membership that the heathen festival of

December 25 was adopted and its name changed to "Christ-mass."

It is not known when this was officially done, but it was not observed as a ritual of the church before the fourth century.

Let us go back now and look at the origins of this wintertime, pagan celebration.

ORIGINS OF THE CHRIST-MASS

To find the origins of the heathenistic custom that we know as Christmas today, we must go all the way back to the city (nation) of Babylon, founded by Nimrod, the *"mighty hunter"* (Genesis 10:8-10). Babylon was the seat of the first great apostasy against God after the Flood. It was here that the Babylonian cult was instituted by Nimrod and his queen, Semiramis. (Semiramis was Nimrod's mother and later his wife, in an incestuous relationship.) From this Babylonian cult is derived all kinds of worship, carried over today into various pagan religions, including the Christ-mass.

The Babylonian cult was a system claiming the highest wisdom and an ability to reveal divine secrets. It was characterized by the word "mystery" because of its system of claimed mysteries. Besides confessing to the priest at admission, a believer was compelled to drink of "mysterious beverages" which, according to Salverte (*Des Sciences Occults*, page 259) was also a requirement for those who sought initiation into these mysteries.

Once admitted into the Babylonian mystery religion, men were no longer Babylonians, Assyrians, or Egyptians, but members of a mystical brotherhood over which was placed a supreme pontiff (or high priest) whose word was final in all matters concerning the lives of the brotherhood (regardless of the country in which they lived). It was, therefore, a supranational organization.

The objects of worship were the supreme father, the incarnate female (queen of heaven), and her son. The last two were the only objects of worship in that it was believed that the supreme father did not interfere in mortal affairs (*Nimrod III*, page 239).

Actually, this system is believed to have had fallen angels and demons as its source. The object of the cult was to rule the world through its dogmas.

THE SPREADING OF THE BABYLONIAN CULT

During the days of Nimrod, this cult gained a deep hold over the whole human race, for there was only one language at that time and all people were one homogenous group. The Bible tells us that Nimrod gained the titles "mighty hunter" and "the apostate" because of his innovative building of walled cities to free men from the ravages of wild beasts (which were then multiplying against mankind) and because of his leading men away from the idea of a God who was capable of interceding with wrath into the affairs of men. History records that he led people astray to such an extent that they drifted from the faith of their fathers.

It appears, from ancient history, that these individuals became involved in the worship of the heavens through the zodiac (astrology) placed atop the Tower of Babel on the plains of Shinar. The end result was that God confused their language and scattered them throughout the earth.

It seems that this Babylonian system was one through which Satan planned to circumvent the truth of God. From Babylon it spread to the ends of the earth — to the place where, Scripture records, Abraham was chosen of God to flee these idolatrous nations and thus preserve the truth of

God. (This would explain how so many different nations of the world are found to have common religious traditions interwoven into their cultures.)

Babylon continued to be the seat of worldwide satanic activity until it was conquered by Xerxes in 487 B.C., when the Babylonian priesthood (the Chaldeans) were forced to move to Pergamos, which then became their headquarters.

Over the years this cult gained power to the point that the Caesars absorbed the bulk of their principles and structure into their own pagan religion. Julius Caesar was made the supreme pontiff of the Etruscan Order in 74 B.C. Thereafter, Rome's religion became that of Babylon.

The Roman emperors continued to hold this office until A.D. 376 when the Emperor Gratian (through Christian motivation) banned it; he saw that Babylonianism was idolatrous by nature. Religious matters then became somewhat disorganized until those in power decided once again to establish this position of apostasy.

ROMAN CHRISTENDOM

In A.D. 378 Damascus, bishop of the Christian church of Rome, was elected to fill this office. He had been bishop for twelve years, having been made such in A.D. 366. This was brought about through the influence of the monks of Mount Carmel, a college within the Babylonian religion founded by the priest of Jezebel and, incredibly, still in existence today within the Roman church.

So, in A.D. 378 the Babylonian system of religion became an official part of the Christian church as it was then constituted. The bishop of Rome, who later became the supreme head of the organized church, was already supreme pontiff of the Babylonian order.

All the teachings of pagan Babylon and Rome were gradually absorbed into the Christian religious organization. Soon after Damascus was made pontiff, the rites of Babylon began to come to the forefront. The worship methods of the Roman Catholic church became Babylonian, and under Damascus (the supreme pontiff), heathen temples were restored and reestablished.

THE EFFECT UPON
ORGANIZED CHRISTIANITY

The changes resulting from this union within the doctrines and practices of the Roman church did not come about all at once. The Roman church of today is purely a human institution. Its doctrines, which frequently stand in opposition to God's Word, were never taught by Christ or the apostles. They crept into the church over a long period of time.

It is evident, to anyone who dispassionately examines the record, that Babylonian rites and practices were inserted into the Roman Catholic church when its major influence became the supreme pontiff of the Babylonian order. In fact, many of today's pagan elements within the Catholic church were taken directly from the Babylonian religion, as founded by Nimrod and Semiramis.

THE WORSHIP OF SAINTS
AND THE VIRGIN MARY

To understand the reasons behind all this, we must examine the situation as it existed throughout Southern Europe toward the end of the fourth century. The official religion, imposed by government edict, was the Christian faith, as then interpreted by officials in Rome, but the mass of the population had for centuries followed the pagan religions. They, therefore, ostensibly accepted the Christian faith (out of necessity), but maintained observance of all the heathen deities, customs, and holidays.

So, to gain a semblance of public compliance with the official religion, it became apparent to the Roman powers that the simplest solution would be to absorb into their Christian format all the pagan elements demanded by the general population. Thus the stage was set for a merging of the Christian and heathen religions.

The populace was accustomed to worshiping a number of gods of various origins and categories (fertility, success in battle, wisdom, etc.). To cater to this custom, the veneration of a wide roster of saints and holy men was instituted. Saints were considered to be lesser deities personally, but who, nevertheless, carried the power to act as intercessors with God. Contrarily, the Bible states:

> *"There is one God, and one mediator between God and men, the man Christ Jesus"* (I Timothy 2:5).

> *"Jesus . . . because he continueth ever, hath an unchangeable priesthood. Wherefore he is able also to save them to the uttermost that come unto God by him, seeing he ever liveth to make intercession for them. For such an high priest became us, who is holy, harmless, undefiled, separate from sinners, and made higher than the heavens; Who needeth not daily, as those high priests, to offer up sacrifice, first for his own sins, and then for the people's: for this he did once, when he offered up himself'* (Hebrews 7:22-27).

Places associated with various holy men were declared sacred, and pilgrimages were instituted. Relics of these officially designated "saints" were believed to have miracle-working powers. When Martin Luther first visited Rome, he expected to see a beautiful city dedicated to the glory of God. What he actually saw revolted and sickened him. Wagons were coming into Rome to the so-called Holy See carrying hundreds of bones and mummified body parts purported to be the remains of saints. Every church could become a holy shrine (that is, holier than other churches) if it contained one of these relics of a saint.

The worship of the Virgin Mary was set up three years after Damascus became head of the Babylon cult, in A.D. 381. Because the Babylonian cult and the general populace worshiped the "queen of heaven" (along with her son), the Roman church saw that it would be politically expedient to supply them with a parallel figure within their new, officially imposed worship. Thus, Mary was elevated to divine status.

The image of mother and child had been a primary object of worship in Babylon for centuries before Christ was born. From Babylon, this had spread to the ends of the earth. The original mother in this tableau was Semiramis, the personification of unbridled lust, licentiousness, and sexual gratification.

In studying the worship practices of other nations, we find an amazing similarity carried out through wide areas and over long periods of time. In Egypt, the mother and child are known as Isis and Horus; in India, as Isi and Iswara; in Asia, as Cybele and Edoius; in pagan Rome, as Fortuna and Jupiter-puer; in Greece, as Ceres with Plutus in arms. In Tibet, China, and Japan, the first Jesuit (Roman Catholic) missionaries were surprised to find the counterparts of the Madonna (Italian name for the Virgin Mary) and her Child worshiped as devoutly as in Rome itself. Shing Moo, "the mother of China," is represented with child in arms and a glory around her head, just as if a Catholic artist had painted her.

These nations trace their common worship from Babylon, before the dispersion in the days of Nimrod. Thus, we see that the worship of Mary (as an integral part of the worship of her Son) is one of Babylonian derivation. There is no suggestion of such worship in Scripture.

THE WORSHIP AND VENERATION OF IMAGES

Prayer to, and the worship of, images was decreed by the Second Council of Nice in A.D. 787. In the ninth century, certain emperors attempted to abolish this pagan practice, but it was so ingrained in the people (and the abolition so resisted by the monks) that the emperors gave up their efforts. In A.D. 869, a synod at Constantinople capitulated (bowed) to public demand, and image (idol) worship — a purely pagan, Babylonian practice — was officially endorsed by the Roman church.

PRIVATE CONFESSION TO A PRIEST

Confession to a priest had progressed from a small beginning in the second and third centuries to an elaborate system by the time of Pope Innocent III in A.D. 1215. It was not, however, officially endorsed until the Council of Trent in A.D. 1551. People were then compelled to confess to a priest at least once a year and do penance according to the degree of sins committed. Without this confession no one had the right to the sacraments.

This was, of course, the same system Babylon had (which bound the people to the priest by fear of exposure or of retribution through divine wrath). This custom is still in force today, forgiveness (salvation) coming from the absolution (forgiveness) of the priest, and then the partaking of Holy Communion.

THE SIGN OF THE CROSS

The sign of the cross had its origin in the mystic "Tau" of the Babylonian cult. This came from the letter "T", the initial letter of Tammuz (Ezekiel 8:14), but better known in classical writings (and even today) as Bacchus. Bacchus was also known as "the lamented one." Actually, this was just one more name for Nimrod, the son of Cush. (Even today Bacchus lives on as the patron saint of such disgusting public homosexual orgies as are evident during the New Orleans Mardi Gras.)

THE ROSARY

The rosary is also of pagan origin. It is used for the same magical purposes in Romanism for which it was used in the Babylonian mysteries. Throughout the Middle East it is common to see Arabs fingering their prayer beads as they sit contemplating in the public bazaars. But Jesus specifically warned against the vain repetition of memorized prayers:

> *"When ye pray, use not vain repetitions, as the heathen do: for they think that they shall be heard for their much speaking"* (Matthew 6:7).

CELIBACY

Also borrowed from the Babylonian cult, the nuns are the reinstitution of the vestal virgins of pagan Rome (copied from Babylon).

Just about all the outstanding festivals of Romanism, such as Christmas, Easter, St. John's Day, Lady Day, Lent, etc. are Babylonian in origin and have been adopted (after application of a thin veneer of Christianity) into the Catholic church despite the fact that they have no relation to Christ or the Bible. None of these were celebrated in Christendom for the first century after Christ. As we have previously explained, they are of pagan origin and were later included into Christian practice as an appeasement to public desires for their old pagan customs.

This is true of Lady Day, observed on March 25. This is the supposed day of the miraculous conception of Mary. Among the heathen this was observed as a festival in honor of Cybele (otherwise known as Semiramis and the mother of the Babylonian messiah, Nimrod). In Rome, Cybele was called Domina (or "lady"); hence, the name Lady Day.

EASTER

It will no doubt come as a surprise to most Christians that Easter also springs from the fountain of Babylon. The word "Easter" has no Christian connections whatever since it derives from "Ishtar," the Babylonian title for "the queen of heaven." It was worship of this woman by Israel that was such an abomination in the sight of God (I Samuel 7:3; Jeremiah 44:18). Round cakes imprinted with the sign of the cross were made at this festival, the sign being the sign of life within the Babylonian mystery religion. This day was observed centuries before Christ and is quite obviously involved in many of the customs connected with the modern celebration of Easter.

Eggs, which play a prominent part in celebrating Easter, were a fertility symbol in heathen nations. One of the fables has to do with "an egg of wondrous size that fell from heaven into the River Euphrates. The fish rolled it to the bank where doves settled upon it and hatched it, and out came Astarte [or Ishtar], the goddess of Easter.''

The word ''Easter'' is used only one time in the Bible (Acts 12:4) and here it is mistranslated. The Greek word here translated as ''Easter'' is translated as ''Passover'' at all other places within the Bible and should be here too.

Lent (observed for the forty days preceding Easter) is also derived from the Babylonian system of mysteries. It is observed today by devil worshipers in Kurdistan, who obtained it from the same source as Rome did: the Babylonian mystery religion. Both Easter and Lent were introduced into the church in A.D. 519.

A writer of this time (Cassianus) said that the observance of Lent had no existence as long as the church remained inviolate. At the same time of the year that Romanism observes it, heathens observe it as the prelude to an entirely different kind of religious observance (''The Rape of Proserpine'') which involves activities of unbridled lust. In their minds, the enforced morality of the Lent season only serves to sharpen their zeal for the degrading activities that will follow.

A great many doctrines and heresies adopted by the Roman Catholic church over a period of centuries actually come directly from pagan sources. Many of the practices thought of today as Christian are, in truth, heathen in origin.

> *''Now the Spirit speaketh expressly, that in the latter times some shall depart from the faith, giving heed to seducing spirits, and doctrines of devils; Speaking lies in hypocrisy; having their conscience seared with a hot iron; Forbidding to marry, and commanding to abstain from meats''* (I Timothy 4:1-3).

HERESIES

While we are on the subject of the major heresies introduced into Christianity through the romance of the Roman church with paganism, it is perhaps a good time to list here a general compilation of current religious practices that stem directly from pagan sources. These various traditions have been inserted into Christianity over a period of more than sixteen centuries. Many of these practices were observed and followed over the years, but only at the times that they were officially adopted (by church councils and then proclaimed by the pope) did they become binding on all Catholics everywhere. These are the dates that will be used here, despite the fact that the traditions and usage might be older than otherwise appears.

At the Reformation in the sixteenth century, when Martin Luther redirected a world's attention (and conscience) to God's Word, these heresies were identified and repudiated as having no part in the religion of the Lord Jesus Christ as taught in the New Testament. Let us list and examine these heresies as they are observed within the Catholic church today.

- Of all the human inventions taught and practiced by the Roman Catholic church that are contrary to the Bible, the most ancient are the prayers for the dead and the sign of the cross. Both of these began about three centuries after Christ, and there is no mention of either within the Word of God.

- Wax candles were introduced into churches *about* A.D. 320. These votive candles supposedly help to bring about prayer requests when paid for, and lighted, in conjunction with prayer.

- Veneration of angels and dead saints began *about* A.D. 375.

- The Mass, as a daily celebration, was adopted in A.D. 349.

- The worship of Mary, the mother of Jesus, and the use of the term "mother of God," as applied to her, originated *about* A.D. 381. This was officially decreed in the Council of Ephesus in A.D. 431.

- Priests began to adopt distinctive costumes *about* A.D. 500.

- The doctrine of purgatory was first established by Pope Gregory the Great *about* A.D. 593.

- The Latin language, as the language of prayer and worship in the church, was imposed by Pope Gregory in A.D. 600 (this has since changed). The Bible teaches that we pray to God alone, in the name of Jesus (John 16:23). In the Early Church prayers were *never* directed to Mary or to dead saints. This practice began in the Roman church about six centuries after Christ.

- The papacy is of pagan origin. The title of pope (universal bishop) was given to the bishop of Rome *about* A.D. 600, from the Babylonian cult (as explained). Jesus did *not* appoint Peter to the headship of the apostles and, in fact, expressly forbade such notion (Luke 22:24-26; Ephesians 1:22, 23; Colossians 1:18; I Corinthians 3:11).

- The kissing of the pope's feet began in A.D. 709. It had been a pagan custom to kiss the feet of emperors. The Word of God forbids such practices (Acts 10:25, 26; Revelation 19:10; 22:8, 9).

- The temporal power of the popes began in A.D. 750. Jesus expressly forbade such a practice and He Himself refused any worldly kingship (Matthew 4:8-10; 20:25-28; John 18:36).

- The worship of the cross, images, and relics was authorized in A.D. 787. Such practices are termed idolatry in the Bible and are severely condemned (Exodus 20:2-6; Deuteronomy 27:15; Psalm 135:15).

- Holy water (water mixed with a pinch of salt and blessed by a priest) was authorized in A.D. 850.

- The canonization (official certification) of saints was instituted by Pope John XV in A.D. 995. Actually, every believer and follower of Christ is referred to as a "saint" in the Bible (Romans 1:7; I Corinthians 1:2; and more).

- The Mass was developed gradually as a sacrifice (of Christ on the cross) and was made obligatory in the eleventh century. The Gospel teaches that the sacrifice of Christ was offered once and for all and is not to be *repeated,* but only *commemorated* in the Lord's Supper (Hebrews 7:27; 9:26-28; 10:10-14).

- The celibacy of the priesthood was decreed by Pope Hildebrand Boniface VIII in A.D. 1079. Jesus imposed no such rules nor did any of the apostles. On the contrary, Peter was married, and Paul stated that bishops (pastors within our terminology) were to have one wife and could have children (I Timothy 3:5, 12; Matthew 8:14, 15).

- The rosary (or prayer beads) was introduced by Peter the Hermit in A.D. 1090. This was copied from the Hindus and Muhammadans. The counting of prayers is a pagan practice and is expressly condemned by Christ (Matthew 6:5-7).

• The inquisition (torture) of heretics (anyone disagreeing with the interpretations coming out of Rome) was introduced by the Council of Verona in A.D. 1184. Jesus, on the other hand, never taught the use of force to spread the Gospel.

• The sale of indulgences, generally regarded as the purchase of forgiveness (for self or for deceased relatives) and a permit for indulging in sin, began in A.D. 1190. The Christian religion, as taught in the Bible, condemns such, and it was primarily protest against this specific abuse that brought on the Protestant Reformation in the sixteenth century.

• The dogma of transubstantiation was decreed by Pope Innocent III in A.D. 1215. According to this doctrine, the priest miraculously changes the communion wafer into the actual body of Christ, which he then proceeds to eat before the congregation. The Gospel condemns such super- stitious absurdities. It clearly stipulates that the act of Holy Communion is a memorial observation of the sacrifice of Christ (Luke 22:19, 20; John 6:35; I Corinthians 11:26).

• The confession of sins to the priest at least yearly was instituted by Pope Innocent III at the Lateran Council in A.D. 1215. To the contrary, the Bible commands us to confess our sins directly to God (Psalm 51; Isaiah 1:18; Luke 7:48, 15:21; I John 1:8, 9).

• The adoration of the wafer (the host) was invented by Pope Honorius in A.D. 1220. The Roman Catholic church thus worships a god made by hands. This is, by scriptural definition, idolatry and absolutely contrary to the spirit of the Gospel (John 4:24).

- The Bible was labeled a forbidden book by the Catholic church (as far as laymen were concerned) and placed in the index of forbidden books by the Council of Toledo in A.D. 1229. Jesus and Paul commanded that the Scriptures should be read by *all* (John 5:39; II Timothy 3:15-17).

- The scapular was invented by Simon Stock, an English monk, in A.D. 1287. This is a piece of brown cloth with a picture of the Virgin sewn onto it and is superstitiously believed to assure salvation, no matter the depth of a person's depravity, if worn next to the skin. This is superstition and fetishism of the most degrading kind!

- The Roman Catholic church forbade the cup (as part of Holy Communion) by instituting communion via the host alone in the Council of Constance in A.D. 1414. The Gospel commands us to celebrate Holy Communion with bread *and* wine (Matthew 26:27; I Corinthians 11:26-29).

- The doctrine of purgatory was proclaimed as a doctrine of faith by the Council of Florence in A.D. 1439. There is not one word in the whole Bible suggesting that such a place as purgatory exists. Acceptance of the blood of Jesus *completely* cleanses of sin and leaves no sinful residue that must be burned off before we may enter the Kingdom (I John 1:7-9; 2:1, 2; John 5:23; Romans 8:1).

- The doctrine of seven sacraments was affirmed in A.D. 1439. The Gospel says that Christ instituted *two* sacraments: Water Baptism and the Lord's Supper (Matthew 28:19, 20; 26:26-28).

- The Council of Trent (covering several years) in A.D. 1545 declared tradition to be of equal authority with the Bible. By tradition was meant human opinions and their teaching. While there is room for *interpretation* of certain aspects of Scripture, there is never room for establishing traditions in opposition to Scripture. The Roman church is saying in this doctrine that when it chooses, it can do anything it wishes in opposition to Scripture and is in no way bound by Scripture. The Pharisees also believed this, and Jesus condemned them with no room for misunderstanding because of their position on this issue (Mark 7:7-13; Colossians 2:8; Revelation 22:18).

- The immaculate conception of the Virgin Mary was proclaimed by Pope Pius IX in A.D. 1854. This doctrine has nothing to do with Mary's conception of Jesus by the Holy Spirit. It says, instead, that Mary was the only human ever born (except Adam and Jesus) without original sin. This implies, therefore, that Mary did not need a Saviour and that she was divine. To the contrary, the Gospel states:

"There is none righteous, no, not one . . . For all have sinned, and come short of the glory of God" (Romans 3:10, 23; compare Romans 5:12).

In the Magnificat, Mary stated that she had need of a Saviour when she referred to Christ as *her* Saviour:

"My soul doth magnify the Lord, And my spirit hath rejoiced in God my Saviour. For he hath regarded the low estate of his hand-maiden" (Luke 1:46-48).

- In 1931 Pope Pius XI reaffirmed the doctrine that Mary is "the mother of God," a doctrine first decreed by the Council of Ephesus in A.D. 431. This heretical statement is contrary to Mary's own words.

In summary, an overwhelming percentage of the rites and ceremonies of the Roman Catholic church are of pagan origin. Cardinal Newman, in his book, *The Development of the Christian Religion* (Catholic), admits that "temples, incense, oil lamps, votive offerings, holy water, holidays and seasons of devotions, processions, blessing of fields, sacerdotal vestments, the tonsures of priests, monks, and nuns, and images, *are all of pagan origin*" (page 359).

IS CHRISTMAS A PART OF THIS?

As mentioned at the beginning of this chapter, Christmas is looked upon in one of three ways: the biblical context, the framework of commercialism, and the perspective of its heathen origins.

If Christmas is observed in the way the Bible presents it, and if we celebrate it with the realization that Christ was not, in all probability, born on December 25 and that we are celebrating His birth *irrespective* of the day on which He was born, then I think we can celebrate it without being contrary to Scripture.

It is not wrong to give gifts to loved ones, but this should not, of course, be paramount or overindulged. Our greatest gift should be to the Lord Jesus Christ, and this should be our love and reverence.

As far as Christmas trees are concerned, I realize that most Christians put little weight to the religious significance of the tree itself, and it is probably little more than a harmless conformation to current customs. Realizing its pagan origins, however, we no doubt would all be better off if this custom had never been allowed to flourish as it has within our society.

To be sure, it is wrong to teach that Santa Claus (or Saint Nicholas) is real. No child should be taught myths about some mystical gift-giver. A child, from the time he is able to understand, should be taught the true meaning of Christmas, which should center on the observance of the birth of Christ.

A child should be taught the truth: no one knows the day Christ was born, but we celebrate His birth on this particular day in spirit because we are thankful to God for His gift beyond price — His Son, Jesus Christ.

> *"For God so loved the world, that he gave his only begotten Son, that whosoever believeth in him should not perish, but have everlasting life. For God sent not his Son into the world to condemn the world; but that the world through him might be saved"* (John 3:16, 17).

> *"For what the law could not do, in that it was weak through the flesh, God sending his own Son in the likeness of sinful flesh, and for sin, condemned sin in the flesh"* (Romans 8:3).

> *"In the beginning was the Word, and the Word was with God, and the Word was God . . . And the Word was made flesh, and dwelt among us, (and we beheld his glory, the glory as of the only begotten of the Father,) full of grace and truth"* (John 1:1, 14).

> *"Thanks be unto God for his unspeakable gift"* (II Corinthians 9:15).

It was Jesus who died for our sins on Calvary when God became flesh and came to dwell among men.

"Jesus . . . made himself of no reputation, and took upon him the form of a servant, and was made in the likeness of men: And being found in fashion as a man, he humbled himself, and became obedient unto death, even the death of the cross. Wherefore God also hath highly exalted him, and given him a name which is above every name: That at the name of Jesus every knee should bow, of things in heaven, and things in earth, and things under the earth; And that every tongue should confess that Jesus Christ is Lord, to the glory of God the Father" (Philippians 2:5-11).

"Jesus . . . was made a little lower than the angels . . . that he by the grace of God should taste death for every man" (Hebrews 2:9).

"Neither is there salvation in any other: for there is none other name under heaven given among men, whereby we must be saved" (Acts 4:12).

On Christmas Day it would be a fine thing if the whole family, particularly the children, would be afforded the opportunity to hear and discuss the Christmas story from the Gospel of Luke. If this were done repeatedly, then our children would come to know the true meaning of this holiday we call Christmas.

It is always Satan's desire to subvert the child of God from the simple truth of biblical worship. Sad to say, he has been successful in this over the years. Hundreds of millions of people are in heathenistic bondage to a super-stitious system that is totally divergent from true salvation. According to the Holy Word of God, salvation comes only through a relationship with Jesus Christ.

Christmas can be beautiful when viewed within the context of God's Word. Otherwise, it becomes little more than a pagan holiday, which I fear has happened in the hearts and lives of the majority of people who attempt to celebrate Christmas. Instead of the frenetic pace of Christ-mas shopping, office parties, and holiday entertaining, if everyone would return to the Word for guidance at this season, we could find that it is indeed possible to worship the Lord Jesus Christ in the beauty of holiness.

> *"And there were in the same country shep-herds abiding in the field, keeping watch over their flock by night. And, lo, the angel of the Lord came upon them, and the glory of the Lord shone round about them: and they were sore afraid. And the angel said unto them, Fear not: for, behold, I bring you good tidings of great joy, which shall be to all people. For unto you is born this day in the city of David a Saviour, which is Christ the Lord. And this shall be a sign unto you; Ye shall find the babe wrapped in swaddling clothes, lying in a manger. And suddenly there was with the angel a multitude of the heavenly host praising God, and saying, Glory to God in the highest, and on earth peace, good will toward men"* (Luke 2:8-14).

Note: *We are indebted to Finis Jennings Dake and his book,* Revelation Expounded, *for much of the information contained herein.*

CHAPTER
ELEVEN

THE SHROUD
OF
TURIN

 will tell you at the outset that the shroud of Turin
is a hoax, but let us look at it a little more closely.
The shroud of Turin is an unlikely object for
serious scientific study or religious edification: it is simply
an old linen cloth, stated by some to be the burial shroud
which Joseph of Arimathaea and Nicodemus draped
around the body of Jesus before they laid Him in the tomb
(John 19:38-40). The cloth is imprinted with an image, but
that image that is ghostly dim.

IT FIRST BECAME KNOWN *ABOUT* A.D. 1357

The shroud of Turin became known *about* A.D. 1357
when it was exhibited in a small wooden church in the
sleepy French provincial town of Lirey, about one hundred
miles southeast of Paris. The shroud's owner, Geoffrey
de Charny, had been killed the previous year by the

English at the Battle of Poitiers. Impoverished by her husband's death, his widow, Jeanne de Charny, hoped to attract pilgrims (and their monetary offerings) by exhibiting in the local church what was purported to be Jesus' burial garment.

No one was ever able to explain how the shroud came into this family's possession. It seems that people in these medieval times did not give any credence to Madame Charny's claims, and it was only when the shroud came into the possession of the powerful House of Savoy that it was accepted in some ways as the true shroud of Christ. It also seems that now, in the twentieth century, some *so-called* scientists accept the shroud's authenticity more readily than it was accepted in the past.

RESEMBLANCE

Supposedly, the image of the face of the man buried in the shroud closely resembles the standard *artists' renderings* of the face of Christ, and it is said that people immediately recognize the image as being the face of Christ — simply and solely *because* it is the standard face of Jesus *in art*.

Around the year A.D. 1464, Pope Sixtus IV let it be known that he regarded the garment as an authentic relic.

In A.D. 1578, the shroud was moved to Turin, Italy. It has remained there since that time except for a six-year period in World War II when it was safeguarded in a remote abbey in the mountains of southern Italy.

I do not personally believe that the shroud of Turin is the burial shroud of Jesus Christ. There are several reasons why I have drawn this conclusion, and I will use the remainder of this chapter to share them with you.

TOO MANY RELICS

I do not know for a certainty that the Catholic church considers the shroud to be genuine. I *do* know, however, that the Catholic church is notorious for coming up with all types of relics, each reported to be some miracle object which, in their thinking, gives some measure of authenticity to the Catholic church.

This was the very thing that caused Martin Luther, when he first saw Rome, to realize that something was amiss in the Catholic church. He expected to view a city ablaze with the glory of God, but instead he saw something that sickened him and turned his stomach.

BONES

As Martin Luther stood on a hill overlooking the city, he saw a multitude of wagons coming in, many of which were filled with bones purported to be the remains of apostles or saints who had died. Any church that could conjure up one of these so-called remains was thought to be more holy than other churches. Thus, the wagons were taking the bones to certain, particular churches. But for all these bones to have been authentic, there would have had to have been several tens of thousands of apostles. So one can readily see the amount of fakery that accompanied all of this activity. This practice has continued through the centuries and is still happening today.

THE MADONNA

The "Madonna" is an object made to look like the Virgin Mary (or rather, what somebody thought the Virgin Mary looked like). Supposedly, at times, it cries real tears.

I was conducting a crusade in Manila (in the Philippines) when the "Madonna" was scheduled to make its appearance in the city. Thousands lined the roadside as the object was carried off the plane and taken on its tour of the city.

These types of sightings and observations are constantly going on within the Catholic church. Most of the time the Catholic priests do not deny them or accept them; they merely "use" them. In other words, each is another relic that is given to the people with a slight suggestion that God gives these types of things only to the "true" church.

Consequently, it would behoove all of us to be suspicious of any type object, relic, or whatever that is purported to be some form of "miracle" coming from the Catholic church. This is certainly not to say that God cannot perform miracles — He is a miracle-performing God — but, at the same time, all of these sightings and observations are spurious indeed. They always have been, and they are today. I believe the shroud of Turin falls into the same category.

THE DISFIGUREMENT OF CHRIST

Jesus took a terrible beating, and, considering the resultant disfigurement from the beating, I seriously doubt that any shroud or cloth would have left any type of identifying marks. The Word of God attests to this:

> *"I gave my back to the smiters, and my cheeks to them that plucked off the hair: I hid not my face from shame and spitting"* (Isaiah 50:6).

Here it says that Jesus' beard was plucked off. This within itself would have caused horrible swelling and disfigurement, as well as some loss of blood.

> *"And they clothed him with purple, and
> platted a crown of thorns, and put it about his
> head"* (Mark 15:17).

It is commonly known that the scalp of a human being
is most tender. If it receives any type of blow or puncture,
it swells almost immediately. We are told that the thorns
used in the makeshift crown that penetrated Jesus' head
were "victors' thorns." These thorns are said to be about
six inches long and are strong and sharp. This type of mat
thrust upon His head, if it was indeed done that way,
would have perforated His scalp and caused tremendous
swelling almost immediately.

Also, we read:

> *"And they smote him on the head with a
> reed, and did spit upon him, and bowing their
> knees worshipped him"* (Mark 15:19).

"They" could have been as many as six hundred men,
as it says they called together the whole "band."

> *"And the soldiers led him away into the hall,
> called Praetorium; and they called together the
> whole band"* (Mark 15:16).

The Greek word for "band" is *speira*, meaning a
company assembled around a standard. It was a whole
company of Roman soldiers, which was usually about six
hundred men. If all of these men — or even a small portion
of them — hit Jesus over the head with a reed, you can well
imagine what this did to Him, considering that thorns were
pressing on His brow and the reed hitting the thorns was
pressing them even deeper. More than likely, His head
swelled far beyond its normal size.

"MARRED MORE THAN ANY MAN"

Scripture says Jesus was marred more than any man:

"As many were astonied at thee; his visage was so marred more than any man, and his form more than the sons of men" (Isaiah 52:14).

The Hebrew word for "marred" is *mishchath*, which carries the idea that in His sufferings the Messiah was so bruised, beaten, marred, disfigured, stricken, mutilated, injured, spat upon, and torn that His outward appearance was terrible to behold. His sufferings were so great that even the most wicked of hardhearted men shuddered with shock at the treatment heaped upon Him. Jesus became so disfigured and destitute of His natural beauty and handsomeness that men were stricken with amazement, disgust, and heartsickness at what they saw. The perfection of His body made the marring He suffered seem even more severe.

Considering all the things that the Word of God says about the terrible disfigurement of Jesus' countenance (visage) and the horrible death He died, it seems highly unlikely that any garment placed upon His face would have left any imprint even remotely resembling that of a human being. It seems from Scripture that Jesus' countenance was grotesque after the pulling of His beard, the placing of the crown of thorns, and the beating upon His head by so many men. Recounting the Scripture that says His visage (face) was *"so marred more than any man,"* I think the evidence is fairly conclusive. Any garment placed over Him would have left no recognizable imprint.

IN CONCLUSION

No, the shroud of Turin is not real. It is but another relic (possibly) produced by the Catholic church to deceive a gullible public into believing that the Catholic church is the true church and that, in some small way, things of this nature add to its prestige and authenticity.

CHAPTER
TWELVE

THE DOCTRINE OF PURGATORY

he Catholic church has defined the existence of purgatory in the Decree of Union drawn at the Council of Florence in A.D. 1439, and again at the Council of Trent, which says:

"The Catholic church, instructed by the Holy Spirit, has from sacred Scriptures and the ancient traditions of the fathers taught in sacred councils and very recently in the ecumenical synod that there is a purgatory, and that the souls therein detained are helped by the suffrages of the faithful, but principally by the acceptable sacrifice of the altar."

The Catholic church also teaches that Christians can indulge in two types of sin — mortal sins (which will damn the soul) and venial sins (which will not damn the soul but will consign them to purgatory). All, therefore, who die in venial sins or with the temporal punishment of their sins still unpaid must atone for them in purgatory.

The Catholic church gets some of her beliefs from apocryphal writings (II Maccabees 12:43-46). Of course, as we have explained, these writings were considered by the Jewish rabbis as unworthy of being included in the Word of God.

The Catholic church goes on to say that because she is the infallible teacher of divine revelation in the name of Bible and tradition, she has the authority to declare the Apocrypha an article of faith in her creeds (the Apostles, the Nicene, and the Athanasian) and in her councils — namely, the Council of Constantinople and the Fourth Lateran Council (in A.D. 1215).

The Catholic church further believes that the faithful on earth, the saints in heaven, and the souls in purgatory are united together in love and prayer. According to her doctrine, the faithful on earth — still struggling to win the victory of salvation — form the "Church Militant" while the saints in heaven are the "Church Triumphant" and the souls in purgatory — still suffering in order to be perfectly purified from the effects of sin — constitute the "Church Suffering."

To sum it all up, the Catholic church states that purgatory is the state or condition in which those who have died in a state of grace, but with some attachment to sin, suffer for a time before they are admitted to the glory and happiness of heaven. In this state and period of passive suffering, they are purified of repented venial sins, satisfy the demands of divine justice for temporal punishment due for sins, and are thus converted to a state of worthiness of the beatific vision.

WHAT DOES THE WORD OF GOD SAY CONCERNING PURGATORY?

Nothing.

All of these teachings are contradicted by the New Testament. We are told . . .

> *"Having therefore . . . boldness to enter into the holiest by the blood of Jesus, By a new and living way . . ."* (Hebrews 10:19, 20).

The Apostle Paul (considering that Paul wrote the book of Hebrews, as we believe he did) taught that where sins are remitted, there is no further need of an offering for sins. Thus Paul concluded his argument on the priesthood of Christ. Christ's offering is efficacious for all past, present, and future sins — but on the condition of proper confession of sin and meeting the terms of continued grace. The Scripture just quoted (Hebrews 10:19, 20) gives the child of God full access to heaven. It is a grand conclusion to the doctrinal argument of the worthiness of every child of God to enter the portals of glory. In other words, *all,* by accepting the blood sacrifice paid for by our Saviour, have instant citizenship in heaven (when God calls us home to be with Him).

It can perhaps be understood how the heathen can teach the doctrine of purgatory as it was taught in Egypt. However, no such excuse can be made for the cardinals, bishops, monsignors, and priests of the Roman Catholic church.

Prayers for the dead go hand in hand with purgatory. In Catholic doctrine, prayer cannot be completely efficacious without the priests as intermediaries, and no priestly functions can be rendered unless there is *special payment* for them. Therefore, in every land we find the priesthood of the Catholic church devouring widows' houses and making merchandise of the tender emotions of sorrowing relatives sensitive to the immortal destiny of their beloved dead.

One of the oppressions under which people in Roman Catholic countries groan is the periodical nature of special devotions for which they are required to pay when death invades a Catholic family. Not only are there funeral services and funeral dues for the repose of the departed at the time of the burial, but the priest pays repeated visits afterward to the family for the same purpose, and this entails seemingly endless heavy expense.

The following is an advertisement which appeared in the August 11, 1946, *Our Sunday Visitor,* a popular weekly Catholic newspaper:

"ARE YOU INSURED?"
Write and ask about our plan to offer the Gregorian Masses after your death. This is real insurance for your soul.

The Gregorian Masses for a soul in purgatory are thirty in number and must be offered consecutively. At that time (1946) the minimum price was $30. It was believed and taught by the Catholics that Christ appeared to St. Gregory and promised He would release souls from purgatory on payment of the money.

I remember years ago in South Louisiana turning on the radio and hearing a particular program hosted by a Catholic priest. He was telling the people to send so much money concerning individuals who had died. He went on to state that all of the body was out of purgatory except an arm, a leg, or some other member. *This is one of the reasons the Roman Catholic church is so rich: the tremendous amount of money pouring into its coffers each day by poor individual Catholics thinking they can retrieve the souls of departed loved ones from a place called purgatory* (that does not, in fact, exist).

The Roman Catholic doctrine of purgatory is purely pagan and cannot for a moment stand in the light of Scripture. The Bible tells us that . . .

> *"the blood of Jesus Christ his Son cleanseth us from all sin"* (1 John 1:7).

On the other hand, for those who die without personal union with Christ and consequently are unwashed, unjustified, and unsaved, there can be no other cleansing.

> *"He that hath the Son hath life; and he that hath not the Son of God hath not life"* (I John 5:12).

Thus the whole doctrine of purgatory is a system of purely pagan imposture, dishonoring God and deluding men who live in sin with the hope of atoning for it after death, thus cheating them out of their property *and* their salvation.

IS PURGATORY REAL?

by Sandy Carson

Editor's note: In the July 1984 issue of The Evangelist, *we ran this article by Sandy Carson, a former Catholic priest. We are so pleased that Sandy has granted us permission to include the article in our book. It is so very timely.*

INTRODUCTION

I am very happy to share with you concerning the subject of purgatory from both historical and biblical perspectives. Let me begin by saying that I was a Catholic priest for seventeen years, serving in the Diocese of Alexandria, Louisiana, from 1955 to 1972. I left the Catholic church and priesthood solely because I came to realize certain contradictions between the Scriptures and Catholic theology. I do not have any bitterness, anger, or resentment toward the Catholic church. However, I do have the conviction that my life and ministry must be squarely based upon the Scriptures, the supreme rule of faith and conduct.

The doctrine of purgatory is a teaching of the Roman Catholic church. It may be defined as an intermediate place or state after death where souls who die in God's grace make atonement, or satisfaction, for past sins and thereby become fit for heaven. This satisfaction is in the form of a temporary punishment which afflicts the soul until the demands of God's justice are fully met. This is in regard to unforgiven venial sins and the punishment still required by divine justice for forgiven sins, whether mortal (sins requiring eternal punishment) or venial (sins requiring some temporary punishment). Catholics readily admit the term "purgatory" is not found in the Bible, but they claim that the factuality of this temporary and intermediate state of cleansing, or purgation, is found in both Scripture and tradition; thus, they claim it as a matter of revelation. Because this place is one of spiritual cleansing, it is theologically called "purgatory"; that is, a place of purgation.

In general, faithful Catholics expect to go to purgatory when they die, as it is believed that almost none die holy enough to enter immediately into heaven. There are exceptions, however. A plenary indulgence (full remission of all temporal punishment due to forgiven sin) can be granted by the church to one who has repented of all sin. It is taught that either a plenary indulgence or martyrdom will take away all punishment otherwise due. In such a case, one would enter heaven immediately upon death.

Once a soul is actually in purgatory it has absolute assurance of entering heaven — eventually. When, no one knows. In the meantime, the faithful on earth may shorten the time a loved one spends in purgatory by obtaining indulgences for them, by having Masses said or offered for them, and by praying for them. Catholics have no assurance their loved ones are really in heaven after death, but they trust they are at least in purgatory. Some Catholics are content to "just get to purgatory," as they believe very few are really good enough to go immediately to heaven.

The subject of purgatory is very much related to that of prayer for the dead. Dealing with one is, in effect, equivalent to dealing with the other. I believe it is best to begin our investigation with official Roman Catholic teaching on these subjects. The basic Catholic teaching will be followed by commentary on it as well as commentary on the church fathers and Scriptures used by the Catholic church to support these doctrines. Finally, I will present a view of these doctrines from the revelaton of Scripture.

OFFICIAL CATHOLIC TEACHING ON
PRAYER FOR THE DEAD AND PURGATORY

General Council of Trent, Sixth Session, Decree on Justification, A.D. 1547, Canon 30:

"If anyone says that after the grace of justification has been received, the guilt is so remitted and the debt of eternal punishment so blotted out for any repentant sinner, that no debt of temporal punishment remains to be paid, either in this world or in the other, in purgatory, before access can be opened to the kingdom of heaven, anathema sit."

("Anathema sit" is a Latin phrase meaning "Let him be cursed." Such a curse is accompanied by excommunication.)

General Council of Trent, Twenty-fifth Session, Decree on Purgatory, A.D. 1563:

"The Catholic church, instructed by the Holy Spirit and in accordance with sacred Scripture and the ancient tradition of the fathers, has taught in the holy councils and most recently in this ecumenical council that there is a purgatory and that souls detained there are helped by the acts of intercession of the faithful and especially by the acceptable sacrifice of the altar . . . ."

Letter of the Sacred Congregation for the Doctrine of the Faith on Certain Questions Concerning Eschatology, May 1979:

"She [Roman Catholic church] believes in the possibility of a purification for the elect before they see God, a purification altogether different from the punishment of the damned. This is what the church means when speaking of hell and purgatory."

SCRIPTURE VERSUS TRADITION:
A COMMENTARY

Canon 30 of the Sixth Session of the Council of Trent is, in fact, a condemnation of biblical truth, as will be shown. Canon 30 also levels a curse against and proclaims the excommunication of those who accept such biblical truth. The Council of Trent's Decree on Purgatory established "there is a purgatory" on the basis of the instruction of the Holy Spirit, on Scripture, and on the tradition of the fathers. This alleged "fact" is indeed found in the "tradition of the fathers," but nowhere in the Scriptures or in the instructions of the Holy Spirit. Certainly, the Holy Spirit would not violate the very Scriptures He Himself inspired.

Also, the Scriptures are not to be judged or added to by the teachings of the church fathers — regardless of their personal reputations for learning and holiness. On the contrary, the writings of the fathers are to be judged by the Scriptures.

The Catholic church falsely claims that the writings of the fathers bear witness to divine revelations not contained in sacred Scripture. Thus, their writings are allegedly a source of "oral tradition," a source of revelation equal to the Bible. However, the Scriptures themselves bear record (inspired as well as historical) that it has been a principle of God from the time of Moses that God's revelation to man is always permanently recorded in written form. This is evident from the following Scriptures: Exodus 17:14; 24:4, 7, 8; Joshua 1:8; 23:6; II Chronicles 34:29-33; 34:21; Mark 7:5-13; I Corinthians 4:6; II Timothy 3:16, 17; 4:1-4; Romans 15:4.

There are many New Testament references to "what is written," showing that the New Testament writers were aware of this principle. Except in II Thessalonians 2:15, the New Testament writers and persons (such as Jesus) never refer to "tradition" as a source of divine revelation. It is always the written Word that is upheld.

The Catholic church uses II Thessalonians 2:15 as Scriptural proof that tradition is a source of divine revelation (Vatican Council II, Dogmatic Constitution on divine Revelation, Chapter 2, No. 8). However, it should be realized that all Scripture was not yet written when Paul exhorted the Thessalonians:

> *"Therefore, brethren, stand fast, and hold the traditions which ye have been taught, whether by word, or our epistle."*

Scripture was not yet written. Likewise, the apostles were channels of revelation, so their oral teaching (tradition) would in no way contradict future New Testament writings. Also, the New Testament revelation ended with the death of the Apostle John, and with his death the written record became finalized and complete. That is to say, with the death of John we have the completion of New Testament revelation as recorded in what has come to be accepted as the New Testament Scriptures.

It must be admitted that the writings of the church fathers (learned and holy leaders in the church of the first seven centuries) at times contradict the plain teaching of Scripture ("prayer for the dead" and "purgatory" being cases in point). Therefore, the "tradition of the fathers" mentioned by the Council of Trent cannot be accepted as a source of divine revelation.

Finally, Jesus recognized the traditions of the Jews for what they were. To the Jew they were equal to *"the commands of God,"* but in reality they were *"rules taught by men"* which served to *"nullify the word of God"* (see Mark 7:7-13). The Christian church fell into the same error as the Jewish church, that of embracing tradition as equal to the written Word in authority. The Scriptures are the sole rule of faith and practice.

A BRIEF LOOK AT THE "TRADITION OF THE FATHERS" USED TO SUPPORT THE DOCTRINES OF PRAYER FOR THE DEAD AND PURGATORY

The following information is taken from the *Dictionary of the Christian Church*, pages 797 and 814.

- *Tertullian* (A.D. 160/70-215/20) was the earliest Father to refer to prayer for the dead. He admitted there is no direct biblical basis for praying for the dead.
- *Clement of Alexandria* (A.D. 150-220) speaks of the sanctification of deathbed patients by purifying fire in the next life. In the early third century church there was much debate over the consequences of post-baptismal sin. A suggested solution was the idea of a purgatorial discipline after death. This concept was discussed at Alexandria, Egypt, at the time of Clement.
- *Augustine* (A.D. 354-430) taught purification through suffering in the afterlife. The concept of purgatory spread to the West — that is, to Italy and West Africa — through the powerful influence of Augustine and Gregory the Great.
- *Gregory the Great* (A.D. 540-604) was Bishop of Rome and therefore Pope from A.D. 590-604. He popularized and developed the doctrine of purgatory, aiding its spread to the West.
- *Thomas Aquinas* (A.D. 1224-1274) also helped to popularize and develop the doctrine of purgatory.

COMMENTARY ON THE "TRADITION OF THE FATHERS"

The Roman Catholic church assumes that the writings, opinions, and theologies of early Christian writers often express divine revelation handed down to them; that is, their writings include teachings of Christ and the apostles which were always a part of revelation but which were never written down under the inspiration of the Holy Spirit as Scripture. Such "truths" make up what is known as "oral tradition" (considered equal to Scripture as divine revelation).

There is no historical or scriptural basis for such an assumption. This is not to say their writings do not express any Christian truth at all, but it is to say they are not the vehicles of revelation — the historical witnesses to revelation — that Roman Catholicism purports them to be. All of their writings must be judged by Scripture, the only bona fide record of actual revealed truth.

The fact is, error began to invade the church at a very early age (the first century, according to the fifteenth chapter of Acts and the book of Galatians). This error came in by way of the backgrounds, or religious heritage (heathen and Jewish), of those who were becoming Christian. As people embraced Christianity, the church unfortunately embraced and "baptized," or "Christianized," some of their false practices (such as praying to the dead; that is, to saints). Second Maccabees is a record of false practice among the Jews of the second century B.C., the practice of praying for the dead "that they may be loosed from their sins" (II Maccabees 12:45). I say this is a record of false practice because it plainly contradicts revelation, as we shall see. It should be noted that II Maccabees (considered as Scripture in the Catholic church, but not considered inspired by Protestants or Jews) is much less historically reliable than I Maccabees, though it covers roughly the same period, 175-134 B.C.

It is interesting to note that Judaism and Islam both embrace the concept of a purgatory in addition to such a concept found in Catholicism. Because it does contradict Christian revelation as determined by the Scriptures, we understand that purgatory is certainly not a Christian concept. The concept of purgatory, therefore, possibly came into the church from a false practice in Judaism (Islam, beginning in the seventh century A.D., may have adopted it from Judaism or Christianity). Likewise, it could have entered Christian doctrine as a theological solution to the "problem" of sins committed after water baptism and the ultimate resolution of the punishment to be endured for them. This undoubtedly had a lot to do with it, since the problem and the *solution* were discussed at Alexandria in the third century. This makes it clear that the doctrine of purgatory does in fact represent man's idea of justice being fulfilled before God. But this is not God's idea or wisdom.

Scripture clearly reveals that *all* the demands of divine justice on the sinner have been completely fulfilled in Jesus Christ. It also reveals that Christ has totally redeemed, or purchased back, that which was lost. The advocates of a purgatory (and the necessity of prayer for the dead) say, in effect, that the redemption of Christ was incomplete.

> *"Neither by the blood of goats and calves, but by his own blood he entered in once into the holy place, having obtained eternal redemption for us . . . For by one offering he hath perfected for ever them that are sanctified"* (Hebrews 9:12; 10:14).

It has all been done for us by Jesus Christ; there is nothing to be added or done by man.

The doctrines of purgatory and prayer for the dead came into the church by way of human teachings and not by the revelation of Christ. Deception is a malady the church has had to contend with even within the first century. Paul was concerned that the church at Colossae might somehow be deceived by *"fine-sounding arguments"* (Colossians 2:4) and he warned that church:

> *"Beware lest any man spoil you through philosophy and vain deceit, after the tradition of men, after the rudiments of the world, and not after Christ"* (Colossians 2:8).

ANTIQUITY AND RESPECTABILITY

Often, in Catholic circles, doctrine is validated by tracing it to the "early days" or "earliest centuries" of the church. It is implied that antiquity is proof of revelation. This is fallacious. We have noted that error crept into the church even in the first century and had to be dealt with. Note that even Peter (Vicar of Christ, head of the church on earth, supreme theologian of the church; i.e., pope — all by Catholic definition) was for a time walking in hypocrisy and outwardly conforming to error until Paul confronted him with the truth (Galatians 2:11-14).

I personally believe that the promotion of certain doctrines by respected and learned men of early centuries (fathers of the church) gave those doctrines the aura of divine revelation. In short, respectable teachers gave false teaching respectability.

It is true that in the mid-fourth century, the Mass was offered for the dead and intercessions for the departed were inserted in the Canon of the Mass. This was simply the amplification of error. Speaking of error, the church knew no concept of an ordained priesthood and "holy sacrifice" of the Mass until the third century. Likewise, such concepts were not universally accepted in the church until the fifth century.

COMMENT ON SCRIPTURES COMMONLY USED TO VERIFY THE CATHOLIC DOCTRINES OF PURGATORY AND PRAYER FOR THE DEAD

• *II Maccabees 12:43-46* (The Apochrypha). The books of Maccabees are not considered inspired outside the Roman Catholic and Greek churches. The inspiration and canonicity of these and other books were in dispute from the time of the African Councils of the late fourth century to the Reformation in the sixteenth century. Accepted by the Jews of Alexandria, Egypt, these books were never accepted by the Jewish scholars of Palestine as belonging to the Jewish Scriptures. Eventually all Jews, including the Alexandrian Jews, accepted a list of canonical books (inspired Scriptures) that excluded the books of Maccabees. The Protestant reformers accepted this Old Testament Canon of the Palestinian (and Alexandrian) Jews.

The Council of Trent (A.D. 1545-1563) retained certain books (Maccabees included) in the Old Testament Canon that had been approved by late fourth century African Councils, but disputed by such notables as Jerome, Cyril of Jerusalem, John Demascene, and Gregory the Great. This demonstrates a long-standing disagreement about these books within the Catholic church. Therefore, II Maccabees 12:43-46 is not considered a scriptural basis for the doctrine of purgatory and prayer for the dead.

• *I Corinthians 3:11-15*. The context of the entire passage indicates that Paul is not speaking of *all men*, but *only* of teachers. The quality of each man's work (teachings) will be judged (fire indicates judgment in verse 13). There are teachers who lead or teach in the wrong direction, but they are right-intentioned, sincere believers, and righteous. Their work may not stand up under God's judgment, but they will not lose salvation (verse 15).

The latter part of verse 15 is variously translated:

> ". . . *he himself will be saved, but only as one escaping through the flames* " (New International Version).

> ". . . *but only as one fleeing through fire*" (New American Bible).

> ". . . *but only as through fire*" (Revised Standard Version).

> ". . . *though rather like a man rescued from a fire*" (Phillips).

> "*he will escape with his life, as one might from a fire*" (New English Bible).

"*Fire*" in verse 15 is a new figure indicating teachers of falsehood will narrowly be saved, as anything or anybody passing through a fire narrowly escapes destruction. We find the same figure used in Amos 4:11 and Zechariah 3:2, which speak of a brand being plucked out of fire.

It is revealing that Paul says all this will happen on Judgment Day, not before (verse 13), thus eliminating any reference to a preceding state of purification between death and "the Day."

In conclusion, I Corinthians 3:11-15 is not a scriptural passage that substantiates a place called "Purgatory." It only says that on the Day of Judgment, some teachers' works will stand and some will not; some teachers of error will be saved even though they were mistaken.

> *"And whosoever speaketh a word against the Son of man, it shall be forgiven him: but whosoever speaketh against the Holy Ghost, it shall not be forgiven him, neither in this world, neither in the world to come"* (Matthew 12:32).

This passage is said to indicate that some lesser sins (venial) will be forgiven after death, thus there is a purgatory where such sins and their due punishments will be taken care of. However, this passage does not substantiate the existence of purgatory, and there are several reasons why.

First, in this passage, Jesus emphasizes that there is no forgiveness for a sin which by nature opposes repentance — which is a gift of God through the Holy Spirit. Mark 3:29 clarifies this, showing that such sin is unforgivable. There is no implication in Mark that some sins will be forgiven after death.

Second, Jesus speaks of *"the age to come."* This is not a reference to purgatory, but to the millennium or possibly life in the Heavenly Jerusalem. Purgatory, in Catholic theology, is a parallel dimension co-existing with our present age on earth.

In summary, the passage teaches that blasphemy against the Holy Spirit absolutely cannot be forgiven under any circumstances.

A SUMMATION OF THE BIBLICAL TEACHING ON THE COMPLETE AND FINISHED WORK OF JESUS CHRIST

The Bible clearly teaches that Jesus Christ, as our substitute, endured the total punishment required to satisfy divine justice on account of our sins. The cost of our salvation was totally paid by Him. Therefore, "purgatory" and the consequent practice of praying for the dead are not only unnecessary, but such theology is a denial that Christ completely redeemed us. Such a theology says that we too must suffer for our sins. Note the following Scriptures.

• *Isaiah, Chapter 53*. This passage (prophetic) shows that the Passion of Christ culminating on the cross was much more than simply a matter of the eternal Son of God infinitely meriting forgiveness of the world's disobedience by His obedience unto death, a death which had infinite value before the bar of divine justice. Redemption (to purchase back that which is lost) involved the price of purchase whereby righteousness is restored to men. So it is that Jesus is described as our *"ransom"* (I Timothy 2:6 and Hebrews 9:15). He paid the *full* price. He was and is the full price, so that by Him we are set free. If that is true, if we are set free, then we are set free from *all* punishment as well as all guilt. One is not free if he still owes a debt of punishment.

How did Jesus qualify as our *"ransom"?* He qualified by His sinless perfection, by His obedience, and by the torturous punishment that He endured because of it. He endured divine wrath as our substitute. This is prophetically affirmed and described in Isaiah 53: He had no beauty (disfigured); He was despised and rejected; He experienced sorrows (pains) and infirmities; He was smitten and afflicted by God, pierced, crushed, wounded, and punished; He bore the iniquity of us all. He was oppressed, stricken, cut off, and killed (assigned a grave); He poured out His life. Isaiah prophesied it.

"He shall see the travail of his soul, and shall be satisfied: by his knowledge shall my

righteous servant justify many; for he shall bear their iniquities'' (53:11).

One justified is also righteous; that is, he has right standing with God. This could not be true if such a one had to personally endure some additional punishment. Again, only Jesus is the Ransom: He paid our total debt.

> *''For he hath made him to be sin for us, who knew no sin; that we might be made the righteousness of God in him''* (II Corinthians 5:21).

Our right standing (righteousness) with God is a gift He imputes to us as a result of faith. We became righteous *''in Him''* and in Him alone, not through our own sufferings, penances, or merits.

> *''But to him that worketh not, but believeth on him that justifieth the ungodly, his faith is counted for righteousness. Even as David also describeth the blessedness of the man unto whom God imputeth righteousness without works''* (Romans 4:5, 6).

It is all in Christ and all a gift, one not merited or achieved by any work, not even by enduring purgatory.
• *Romans 3:21-26.* This passage clearly says righteousness is totally from God as a gift, not as a result of any of our works (including suffering in purgatory). One would not have the right standing (righteousness) before God if he still owed Him some debt of punishment. Again, righteousness is the result of faith in Jesus Christ alone. There is no place for purgatory.

Verse 25 says that Jesus is a *''propitiation through faith in his blood.''* That is:

"Christ through His expiatory death is the personal means by whom God shows the mercy of His justifying grace to the sinner who believes" (W. E. Vine).

This sacrifice also releases the believer from the infliction of any punishment because it is said the sacrifice met all the demands of divine justice: *". . . he did it to demonstrate his justice . . . ."* This reveals that divine justice was completely fulfilled on Calvary's cross. This fulfillment of divine justice is personally realized for the sinner when he has "faith in Jesus" (verse 26) and becomes a believer.

> *"There is therefore now no condemnation to them which are in Christ Jesus, who walk not after the flesh, but after the Spirit"* (Romans 8:1).

There is no judgment against the believer. Scripture nowhere supports the teaching that a sinner can be forgiven guilt and still be held responsible for enduring certain punishment to completely satisfy divine justice. Punishment is eliminated when guilt is forgiven because Jesus Christ endured it all on our behalf.

COMPLETE FORGIVENESS

Scripture makes it clear that when God forgives, our sins are blotted out. When something is blotted out, there is no remaining evidence of it (Psalm 51:9); they are as far away as east is from west (Psalm 103:12); they are behind God's back (Isaiah 38:17); they are remembered no more (Isaiah 43:25). Forgiveness renders one innocent because He is just. The Catholic theology on sin, forgiveness, penances, and purgatory represents a perversion of justice because it advocates the punishment of the innocent. If

God required the forgiven innocent to endure temporary future punishment, the Scriptures just mentioned would not be true.

IN CONCLUSION

I trust this treatment of the subject of purgatory will be of profit to you. It is really comforting to realize that *all* the requirements of divine justice for our sins have been fulfilled in Jesus Christ. His gift of salvation is full and complete, requiring no additional deeds, penances, merits, or sufferings on the part of those who are repentant and believing, accepting Him as Lord and Saviour of their lives (John 3:15-17; 6:47; Romans 10:1-13; Ephesians 2:8-9).

> *"Thanks be unto God for his unspeakable gift"* (II Corinthians 9:15) — the Lord Jesus Christ!

The following sources were used in the composition of this article: *Dictionary of the Christian Church* (Zondervan), *New International Commentary* (Eerdmans), *Matthew Henry's Commentrary* (Zondervan), *Tyndale's New Testament Commentaries* (Eerdmans), *The Expositor's Bible Commentary* (Zondervan), *History of the Christian Church* by Philip Schaff (AP & A), *The Christian Faith in the Documents of the Catholic Church* (Alba House), *The Sixteen Documents of Vatican II* (St. Paul Editions), *Expository Dictionary of New Testament Words* (Revell).

CHAPTER THIRTEEN

THE TRUE CHURCH?

OT A POPULAR ISSUE

We are, sad to say, living in an age when people have little interest in exposing false doctrines. The general spirit of our time is, "Anything goes. Live and let live."

Just the other day, I heard a preacher telling his television audience that sin shouldn't be preached, it shouldn't be defined, it shouldn't be discussed.

Why?

Because no one should be made to feel guilty. He went on to say that we should love everyone because "God is love."

Naturally, we *are* to love everyone. God is undeniably a God of love. The question must be raised, however: *what is love?*

Am I not demonstrating love to my Catholic brethren when I warn them of impending doom if they persist in following the erroneous teachings of the Catholic church?

Is it a failure in love if you warn someone that the bridge is out as·they speed toward it?

Was Jesus cruel when He warned His disciples against the leaven of the Pharisees?

I cannot help but wonder what kind of preacher Jesus was, as His message is quoted in Matthew 23. He used some extremely strong and uncompromising language in this chapter. How would He be accepted by the general public today? Not well at all, I am afraid.

The reason so few preachers are willing to say anything controversial today is no doubt the reaction they will elicit from the entrenched religious establishment. No one likes to be vilified or held up to ridicule. It is so much easier to talk about love, while very little real love is shown. It is so much simpler just to avoid the truth.

In this book on Catholic tradition, I have literally bent over backwards to ensure that every statement is true. My information has come primarily from former Catholic priests. And someone once said that testimony against one's self is the most damning testimony of all. This is the type of testimony we have been presenting throughout this book.

I love the Catholic people. I've stated this over and over again. And even though many of my Protestant friends have taken me to task for trying to call attention to the loss of hundreds of millions of souls, I can only say this:

LOOK AT THE RESULTS!

I believe, without fear of contradiction, that we are seeing tens of thousands of Catholics saved. Oh, there has been a price to pay, but we have paid it — and continue to pay it — gladly in view of the results. To be frank, I am no longer my own — I am bought with a price. I am a bondservant of Jesus Christ, and I must do what He tells me. Therefore I have no choice or alternative. To be frank, I seek none.

THE CATHOLIC CHURCH IS IN A QUANDARY

The majority of today's Catholics accept their designation as Catholic simply because they don't know what else to do. They are in a quandary over many of the dogmas of the Catholic church, so they end up accepting the beliefs that appeal to them while discarding the rest.

Many of those who call themselves Catholic Charismatics try to embrace Pentecostal principles with one hand and Catholic tradition with the other. As a result, they never know which is correct and end up playing both ends against the middle. The primary reason for this confusion in the worldwide Catholic organization is the widespread proliferation of the Word of God over the last few decades.

Many Catholics have been exposed to the Bible for the first time. They are starting to watch telecasts that deliver the true Word. They are learning (to their dismay) that most Catholic doctrines are in total disagreement with the Word of God.

Their priests constantly tell them that the Word of God is to be interpreted only by the bishop or the priest because the ordinary Catholic doesn't have the knowledge to do this on his own. This fragile attempt at dissuasion is rapidly becoming less effective, however. The ache, the void, the emptiness still lies in the hearts of most Catholics.

Way down deep inside they know that something is wrong — seriously wrong — with the teachings of their church. Knowing this, they look off to one side and see the

Protestant denominations. And in many cases, these are no better than what they have.

When they finally glimpse the true light of the Gospel of Jesus Christ, however, they find that they face many new problems. The price is high. Many are willing to pay, but do not know if they have the strength to persevere in their new commitment. But other tens of millions of Catholics say, "If what I believe is wrong, that is the priest's responsibility. It is not my fault."

Unfortunately, this is what they are taught. But here, too, there is a void and a yearning that no rationalization can remove. They might convince themselves on the surface, but deep down they *know* it is their decision.

THREE QUESTIONS

We want to look at three areas in this closing chapter:
• Is the Catholic church the true church in the world today?
• Why do millions of people believe that the Catholic church is the true church?
• What *is* the true church of the Lord Jesus Christ?

IS THE CATHOLIC CHURCH THE TRUE CHURCH IN THE WORLD TODAY?

The contention that our Lord Jesus Christ established the Roman Catholic church as it exists today is a total fabrication.

The apostolic Early Church could well bear the title of "catholic" or "universal" because it included all true Christians. But soon, heated disputes arose over the authority of the bishops, and the originally homogenous church began to splinter. Some churches rallied behind the bishop of Rome, others to the patriarch of Constantinople

— while still others remained independent of either jurisdiction.

To make the salvation of the soul dependent on submission to some particular religious organization is, of course, ludicrous. Christ never uttered a word authorizing such a contention. *The salvation (or loss) of the soul is not dependent on external acceptance of some church, but on a soul-changing belief that forever alters the conscience and the life.* Deviation from the doctrines received by divine inspiration is a grave sin, not only for the religious authorities who promote this, but for every believer as well.

For this reason, unity within the Christian church will remain an impossibility for as long as there is deviation from the teaching of Christ. Any sincere Christian will sacrifice all considerations of community acceptance and church tradition before he will relinquish his faith-inspired knowledge of God's ways.

A sincere Christian, convinced that the salvation of his soul depends on adherence to God's Word, will affirm with the apostles (as they stood before the supreme ecclesiastical court of their day):

> *"Then Peter and the other apostles answered and said, We ought to obey God rather than men"* (Acts 5:29).

Two imposing forces are combined to produce the Roman Catholic type of Christianity. As I read the other day, it was a mixture of evangelical doctrines (as preached by our Lord and His apostles) combined with a pagan sacerdotal religion.

Someone else said that error always rides into the church on the back of truth, which is another way of describing the same situation.

You see, this corruption took place, little by little, over many years. Dilution of the Christian faith came about slowly, but the major impetus was the absorption, by imperial decree, of the entire pagan population of the Roman Empire into the Christian church. These individuals missed the pomp and pageantry of their pagan churches and demanded return of the rites and ceremonies performed within their cults. To satisfy this widespread demand, these rituals and customs were transplanted to the *Christian church* and given disguise under Christian labels.

Gradually, all the great doctrines of the faith were changed and new dogmas (ones always favorable to the material interests of the church) were introduced. These dogmas solved a temporary problem as they quelled the discontent of the masses, but they severely damaged the purity of the faith.

So the question is: Is the Catholic church the authentic church of Jesus Christ? And if it isn't, what church has more right to claim this title?

THE ROMAN CATHOLIC CHURCH IS A POWERFUL, BUT HUMAN, ORGANIZATION

No one denies this fact. If Revelation, Chapter 17, is a description of the Roman Catholic church (as many Bible scholars teach), then it is clear just *why* it is so powerful.

Here we have a description of a huge world system which has attained vast power and riches by entering into base alliances with the political powers of the earth — and which, for a long time, dominated kings according to her whim. She shed much blood in persecutions. Then, in Revelation, Chapter 18, we are told:

*". . . Come out of her, my people, that ye be
not partakers of her sins, and that ye receive not
of her plagues"* (verse 4).

Whether John, the great revelator, was speaking of the
then-still-futuristic Catholic church, I cannot say with
certainty. However, whether he was or was not, the
description certainly fits. And I believe this command by
God is as valid today as on the day it was spoken: *"Come
out of her, my people."*

The Catholic church teaches that she is the true church
of the Lord Jesus Christ on this earth, that she is the
successor to the apostles — and especially to Simon Peter.
She teaches, basically, that one must be associated with
her in some way to be saved.

Still, during the Second Vatican Council, the Catholic
church evasively admitted there was the possibility that
some non-Catholics *might* be saved — although they did
not specify in what way this unlikely circumstance might
be brought about.

The Catholic route to salvation is nebulous — it is a
salvation of works. Faith is mentioned in passing and
deferred to, but in practice it is the priest in whom you
must have faith. Unfortunately, this ends up a matter of the
blind leading the blind. As our Lord pointed out in Luke
6:39, in such cases your inevitable destination is the ditch.

On the other hand, *we state that the Catholic church is
not the true church of the Lord Jesus Christ on earth and
that it has no resemblance to His church.*

Now why do we say this?

*Because the traditions of the Catholic church have
absolutely no basis or grounding in the Word of God.* And
this, of course, must be the true foundation and standard
for all pertaining to God. Regrettably, the Catholic church
just doesn't pass this test.

WHY DO MILLIONS BELIEVE THAT THE CATHOLIC CHURCH IS THE TRUE CHURCH?

There are nearly 800 million nominal Catholics in the world.

As previously stated, many of these are not practicing Catholics. There are perhaps only about 100 million *devout* Catholics in the world, still a considerable figure. But tens, and even hundreds, of millions of Catholics are so in name only. If they attend church at all, it is only once or twice a year.

They pay scant allegiance to their priests or to their traditions, yet they are included within this vast membership of nearly a billion souls. There is no salvation within the Catholic church, and yet millions (perhaps even hundreds of millions) swear allegiance to it.

Why?

BORN INTO IT

Many do so because they were born into the Catholic church. They know nothing else. They have had little or no opportunity to hear the Word of God, so they accept what they *do* hear. (However, this is rapidly changing as the Gospel is being brought before the world via television. As a result, millions of Catholics are beginning to ask questions.)

NO REPROACH

Uncounted numbers elect to stay where they are because there is no reproach to being a Catholic. Committed Christianity carries a reproach. Catholicism is widely accepted throughout the world today, especially in Latin countries.

LOVE DARKNESS

A person does not have to reject sin to be a good Catholic. He can, instead, confess his sins — and then keep right on committing them. Consequently, the Bible observes that *"men loved darkness rather than light"* (John 3:19).

PEER PRESSURE

Millions of Catholics fear the social consequences of abandoning the faith of their families and their social peers. (In certain ethnic neighborhoods, the Catholic church is the center of social activities.)

REBELLION

And many Catholics, sad to say, simply rebel against God (even though they know better) by demanding their "own" religion.

WHAT IS THE TRUE CHURCH OF THE LORD JESUS CHRIST?

The true church of the Lord Jesus Christ is *not* a human organization which is arranged and supported by worldly powers and which is sustained and nourished by secular influences.

The true church of the Lord Jesus Christ is the total company of true Christians of all churches and all times.

Its head is not in Rome, Constantinople, Washington, or any other place. He sits at the very right hand of God.

> *"And what is the exceeding greatness of his power to usward who believe, according to the working of his mighty power, Which he wrought in Christ, when he raised him from the dead, and set him at his own right hand in the heavenly places"* (Ephesians 1:19, 20).

The Lord Jesus Christ (head of the church) said:

> *"For where two or three are gathered together in my name, there am I in the midst of them"* (Matthew 18:20).

This means that there are hundreds, thousands, or millions of churches with no national or international affiliation. The *true* church — the church that is faithful to the Lord Jesus Christ, sincere, and loved of the Lord (and, generally, persecuted of men) — has existed throughout the centuries.

The true church has an unbroken continuity that exists *not* by the imposition of hands — as the church of Rome teaches. How many times has that so-called "continuity of the church" been broken — as even the very Canon of the Roman church itself reveals — because of unworthy links in the succession? That is, by bishops, priests, and popes who have consecrated unworthy successors who didn't fulfill the requirements of intent and conduct.

To the contrary, the continuity of the true church of the Lord Jesus Christ bears the stamp of the Holy Spirit — instilling the same faith, courage, and confidence in its faithful martyrs of all centuries.

The true church has carried a variety of names over the years. In God's view, it is made up of the sons of God. These sons can claim only one merit, and this is that they have obeyed their hearts, rejecting the doctrines of men and accepting instead those God has revealed in His Holy Word.

FIRST-CENTURY CHRISTIANS WERE BELIEVERS IN CHRIST — NOT ROMAN CATHOLICS

First-century Christians did their best, according to the Word of God, to *"contend for the faith which was once delivered unto the saints"* (Jude 3).

They were convinced that they were defending the truth of God, the whole truth, as it was found in the Old Testament — which was then called "Memories of the Apostles." In all discussions — with both pagans and heretics — they turned to these writings as their only source of religious authority.

When they died by the tens of thousands in the Roman arenas, they didn't do so for the Roman Catholic church (whose dogmas have been elaborated through the later centuries). They died instead for the simple, evangelical faith of the New Testament.

THE SAINTS AND THE MARTYRS

Roman Catholics choose to claim all early saints as their own. "Protestantism has no saints, no miracles, no martyrs," they like to observe, "like those of the Roman Catholic church."

Well, let us look at this contention.

For the first three centuries, the Roman Catholic church didn't exist. All the miracles and martyrs of the Early Church (as recorded in the book of Acts) belong exclusively to the Christian church.

We would like to challenge the Catholic church to demonstrate that the saints and martyrs of the first three centuries accepted the beliefs and practices of the Catholic church as it exists today.

They *claim* that the great standard-bearers and witnesses of the early Christian truths (St. Clement, St. Ignatius, St. Theophilus, St. Polycarp, St. Iranaeus, and St. Gregory, among others) were Roman Catholic in faith.

They were not. They had absolutely no resemblance to, nor connection with, what is now known as Roman Catholicism. Their beliefs were according to the New Testament which, we once again emphasize, has no association with Roman Catholic dogma.

Looking at the Early Church, we observe that they fashioned no images of saints. We can look in vain in the catacombs or in the oldest churches for such artifacts. Neither did they kneel before any such idols while offering prayers.

There is no hint in the Word of God that the early saints ever prayed to the Virgin Mary, sought her intercession, or recited prayers to her.

There is no indication in the Early Church that sins were confessed to a priest. There were no Masses offered for the dead. They bought and sold no indulgences, and there is no hint that the bishop of Rome was infallible.

No, *all* of the Early Church fathers were evangelical and Pentecostal and had no association with what is now recognized as the Roman Catholic church. To be frank, as we've stated many times, *there was no such thing as a Roman Catholic church during the first three hundred years after the Lord's ascension.*

THE ORIGIN OF PROTESTANTISM

In the second century, a loose federation of churches came into being with a common code of beliefs which were expressed in confessions much like the Apostles'

Creed. They all utilized a common form of church government. The churches in this federation called themselves the Catholic church — Catholic meaning universal. I hasten to add, however, that they had no resemblance whatsoever to Roman Catholicism as it is known today.

Even at this time there were many churches differing from the Catholic church in belief and organization. The statement of faith had become the test of membership. Soon, individuals were required to document their Christianity by accepting a specific church doctrine — not by their submission to Christ.

With Constantine as emperor, the churches became so standardized that they could be approached as a single organization.

A segregation between the clergy and laymen — unknown in the apostolic age — developed. Bishops, presbyters, and deacons were elevated far above the church members. As a sacrificial connotation became attached to the Lord's Supper, the clergy came more and more to be called "priests."

The office of bishop (originally, pastor) gradually magnified until the bishops became convinced that they had authority to establish doctrine. The idea gradually developed that the clergy should practice celibacy, and when several churches were established in one town, it was felt that they should be under a common bishop. Naturally, the bishops of larger towns assumed more status than those of the smaller dioceses.

In the fifth century, Augustine promulgated his doctrine of the nature of the Catholic church — which was generally accepted. He taught that the first bishops of the church were appointed by the apostles, who had received the gifts of the Holy Spirit from Christ for the care of the church. These, in turn, passed this on to *their* successors — the first bishops — and these successors protected the original faith. They could define Christian practices which would provide salvation.

And thus came the idea that only in the Catholic church was there apostolic succession — which was the mechanism for delivering salvation. Augustine was not the first to teach this, but he worked diligently for its acceptance.

Not so many years passed before true Christians *had to become* Protestants. They were Protestants because they protested the areas that were beginning to pervert the so-called "Great Churches of Christianity." These churches crystallized into an ecclesiastical organization which soon became known as the Roman Catholic church.

Martin Luther was not the first Protestant of the Christian church. There have been a considerable number of them in all the centuries of Christianity.

In the fourth and fifth centuries, true Christians had to protest against the leniency of certain bishops (and, in particular, those of Rome with its corrupt hierarchy).

ST. HIPPOLYTUS

One of these early protesters was St. Hippolytus, in the third century, who protested that the bishop of Rome (whose name was Calixtus) had filled the church with adulterers, murderers, and swindlers — admitting them without any change in heart or life.

THE DONATISTS

In his book, *To the Fountain of Christianity*, Samuel Vila tells of the Donatists — who protested against the introduction of error into the church. They tried to form churches that would return to the truth of sacred Scripture. They suffered terrible persecution as they separated themselves from the organized church.

THE PAULICIANS

In the seventh century there were the Paulicians — who held the writings of St. Paul to be the guiding criteria for Christianity. They had a tremendous influence on the people as they fought desperately against the pagan customs and doctrines creeping into the Roman Catholic church.

Strangely enough, the Greek priest Simon — who had been commissioned to persecute these wayward sheep and incorporate them into the Roman Catholic fold — was moved by their fidelity and converted to their faith. He subsequently became the successor to the very man he had slain. (This was a situation remarkably similar to that of Saul of Tarsus.)

During this time, the Roman Catholic church (according to Empress Theodora) slew with the sword, or burned at the stake, 100,000 of these evangelical Paulicians in the space of nine years.

THE WALDENSES

These people lived in the eleventh and twelfth centuries. Thousands of them died for the cause of Christ. On one occasion in Genoa, 114 Waldenses were burned alive. They were known for their fervent piety and holiness in life, qualities that were even recognized by the Roman Catholics who persecuted them for their doctrinal differences.

THE ANABAPTISTS AND OTHERS

The Anabaptists were individuals who rebaptized all of the hundreds of thousands who had been baptized as infants in the false hope that water baptism somehow conveyed salvation. And later there came the Mennonites and the Plymouth Brethren.

Even though we have merely scratched the surface on the multiplied millions who over the centuries *"contended for the faith once delivered unto the saints,"* I think we have presented enough to disprove the Roman contention that Martin Luther sired the evangelical church. The formation of the evangelical church had been an ongoing struggle from the beginning. Today, although bloated and distended, the Catholic church wields only a shadow of its former power.

There are more true children of God and real Christians today than at any time in history. But a fearful price has been paid.

CHRISTIAN MARTYRS

Only God knows the number of faithful Christians who were murdered at the hands of the Roman Catholic church. We have only to turn the pages of history to be convinced. Through the papal inquisition, multitudes of believers disappeared.

It was with a thrill of horror that Europe heard of the opening of the dungeons of the Inquisition in Spain. The population was enraged when, breaking into the monasteries, they found barely recognizable humans chained to walls. They were stark naked with long, matted hair and nails like claws. Some were quite mad, and others became insane when brought into the light.

The Roman Catholic church has, in the past, been bold in her boast of using her secular arm to punish all heretics — that is, until the nations rebelled and declined to further punish and repress heretics.

Equally bold are the current statements declaring that if they ever regain control, all heretics must recant — or suffer excommunication and death.

THE SAD FACT IS THIS

The Roman Catholic church has changed the substance of the greater part of the teachings and doctrines of the Lord Jesus Christ. These teachings were faithfully observed by the early Christians. When any doubt or question arose, their only approved avenue was to *"search the scriptures"* (John 5:39).

It must be understood that no church organization or individual has the authority to change by as much as a comma the teachings of Christ. The apostles and church fathers would be horrified to see the changes that the Roman Catholic church has instituted in the Word of God.

It should also be noted that the changes which were instituted by the Roman Catholic church (opening the gate of the Kingdom through priestly absolution, sacraments, and indulgences) have no basis in Scripture.

Even though the ceremonies performed by priests are done in good faith, they only fulfill human teachings — and, as such, are worthless when they don't coincide with the teachings of Christ.

Consequently, all hopes that the Roman Catholic may place in these avenues to salvation lack substance. Those trusting in rituals will be shattered on the day they must stand before the Supreme Judge.

Confidence in salvation is the hallmark of the true Christian. You can see this in the New Testament and in the writings of the early Christians. Uncertainty and fear, on the other hand, are the marks of false religions. *The leaders of these false religions like to keep their devotees*

in continuing anxiety and coincidentally reap maximum
material gain from their ecclesiastical services.

FAITH AND WORKS

Salvation, according to the Catholic tradition, is built
on a religion of works. Salvation, according to the Word of
God, is built on faith.

> *"For by grace are ye saved through faith;*
> *and that not of yourselves: it is the gift of God:*
> *Not of works, lest any man should boast"*
> (Ephesians 2:8, 9).

Does this mean then that good works are unimportant?
Of course not. However, works are not a mechanism for
obtaining salvation; they are the result of the spiritual
transformation that comes *with* salvation.

It is not good works that save us, but faith in Christ
manifesting itself in good works. The more real and vital
the faith, the greater the number of works. Further, while
the number of good works has no influence on salvation,
they do determine our heavenly reward. As the Lord
teaches, even a cup of cold water given for the love of
Jesus will not lose its reward (Matthew 10:42).

WE CONTEND THIS

Only the true Christian faith, based on the Word of
God, is capable of producing a conscientious, joyful, and
vital Christian life. This is understandable when we bear in
mind that the true Christian lives a life of satisfaction and
peace for the following reasons:

The true Christian, with his salvation based securely
on the Word of God, is sure of his salvation and, therefore,

of eternal life. Should death threaten him at any moment, he can accept it without fear.

He feeds his soul each day on the sacred Scriptures. Here he daily discovers new promises he can apply to his life situations.

He prays rational prayers to God Almighty in the name of Jesus. He does not parrot vain repetitions but rather addresses himself to God with the frankness and intimacy of a son (or daughter) to a father.

Every act of service for Christ fills him with intense joy — because it springs from love and not from fear. It is his aim to please the One who saved him rather than to accumulate "brownie points" in order to avoid some future punishment.

The vision that the true Christian has of the life beyond is brilliant and enrapturing because of its promised joy — the thought of eternal life in the presence of Christ. In addition, he can anticipate recompense for every good act carried out while he is here on earth. As the Saviour says:

> *"If any man serve me, let him follow me;*
> *and where I am, there shall also my servant be:*
> *if any man serve me, him will my Father*
> *honour"* (John 12:26).

Jesus also promises, concerning the good deeds of the true Christian:

> *"Well done, thou good and faithful servant:*
> *thou hast been faithful over a few things, I will*
> *make thee ruler over many things: enter thou*
> *into the joy of thy lord"* (Matthew 25:21).

Someone said a long time ago, "It is worth being a Christian, with such promises." These promises are, however, nothing more or less than the conditions of the Bible.

It is Christ who declares them and assures us that they are so. And when compared to His infallible Word, the words of men are of little worth — whatever their ecclesiastical prominence.

"IF I AM A CATHOLIC, WHAT MUST I DO?"

• Obtain a copy of the Holy Word of God (preferably in the King James Version) to verify for yourself the promises of God.

• Read the Word of God. See what the Lord and His apostles have to say to you. Believe what you read, and ask God to help you understand it. It is not enough to accept as a historical fact that Jesus lived, died, and rose again. It is necessary to believe His Word, to have confidence in it, and to apply it in your life.

• Present yourself to God in trust and say to Him, "Lord, I believe what You tell me, that I am a great sinner and that I am lost. I know in my heart that no man can grant me pardon, but that You can and You will. But first, I must come unto You of my own free will."

Romans 10:9, 10 is the scriptural passage where we find this promise of salvation and what we must do to receive it:

"That if thou shalt confess with thy mouth the Lord Jesus, and shalt believe in thine heart that God hath raised him from the dead, thou shalt be saved. For with the heart man believeth unto righteousness; and with the mouth confession is made unto salvation."

Romans 10:13 repeats God's promise of salvation, a promise given to all men:

"For whosoever shall call upon the name of the Lord shall be saved."

• Forgive all who have trespassed against you — asking God to help you to do so. Seek to demonstrate your forgiveness by some kindly deed and explain that your action springs from your conversion to Christ — who commands you to do thus.

• You should make a habit of not only reading your Bible every day, but seeking the Lord in prayer. Thank Him for your assurance of salvation, and ask Him for His guidance and that His will be done. If you do so, you will see your prayers answered.

• Ask God to give you the Holy Spirit. It is He who leads men into all truth . . .

"Howbeit when he, the Spirit of truth, is come, he will guide you into all truth" (John 16:13).

"But ye shall receive power, after that the Holy Ghost is come upon you" (Acts 1:8).

With this power of the Holy Ghost, you will sense a revelation of Jesus Christ previously unknown. Offer all your prayers to God in the name of the Lord Jesus Christ, praying to God alone. He is infinite and only He can hear you.

• It will not be necessary to ask you to abandon the superstitious practices of the Roman Catholic church. Your conscience will disclose the enormous contrast between these and the clear and simple teaching of the Word of God.

• Do your best to find a church that believes in salvation by faith and in the mighty baptism in the Holy Spirit. This will be a church that wins souls. You should attend its services and become allied with its people, taking the Gospel of Jesus Christ throughout the world.

• Do not hide the treasure of your discovery of the Gospel of Jesus Christ. Renounce all connections with your past and seek to let others share in that which God has given you. In this, you will fulfill Christ's command to take the Good News to every creature.

THE CONSEQUENCES

You may be vilified, despised, and even threatened. But remember, Christ was despised and suffered far beyond anything you will have to face.

> *"Believe on the Lord Jesus Christ, and thou shalt be saved"* (Acts 16:31).

Put the teachings of our Lord into practice and show through your life that your faith is real.

May God shed His light in your soul and give you grace as you now embark upon the true Christian life.

Bibliography

Babylon Mystery Religion, Ralph Woodrow (Riverside, CA: Ralph Woodrow Evangelistic Association, Inc., 1983).

Catholicism, Richard P. McBrien (Minneapolis, MN: Winston Press, 1970).

"The Catholic Response," Peter M.J. Stravinskas, *Our Sunday Visitor,* Huntington, IN, 1985.

Christ Among Us: A Modern Presentation of the Catholic Faith, Anthony Wildhelm (Paulist Press).

The Cyclopedia of Biblical, Theological, and Ecclesiastical Literature.

Dogmatic Constitution on Divine Revelation, Vatican II, 1965.

Fountain of Christianity, Samuel Vila (Long Island, NY: Christ's Mission, Inc., 1959).

Ineffabilis Deus, Pope Pius IX, December 8, 1954. (Reaffirmed *Decree on Original Sin,* Council of Trent, Session V, 1546.)

La Popessa, Paul I. Murphy (Warner Books).

Munificentissimus Deus, Pope Pius XII, 1950.

Night Journey from Rome to the New Jerusalem, Clark Butterfield (P.O. Box 1513, Upland, CA 91785: Agapesofia Oikoumene, AIC International Christian Ministries).

Pilgrimage from Rome, Bartholomew F. Brewer (Greenville, SC: Bob Jones University Press Inc., 1982).

The Priest: His Dignity and Obligations, St. John Eudas, 1685. (Reissued under the imprimatur of Cardinal Spellman, 1946.)

Providentissimus Deus, Pope Leo XIII, 1893.

The Spouse of Christ, St. Alphonsus Maria de Liguori.